Glaswegiana

William W. Barr

RD

RICHARD DREW PUBLISHING
6 CLAIRMONT GARDENS
GLASGOW G3 7LW
SCOTLAND

To HELEN STUART STEVENSON, Baroness of Kilbride, daughter of the last laird of Castlemilk and in direct line of the Scottish Kings, who owned the ancient estate and mansionhouse of Castlemilk, now one of the largest housing estates in Glasgow and who was of great encouragement and assistance to me in my research.

First Published in 1973
Copyright © William W Barr
First Richard Drew Edition 1980
New edition 1988
Reprinted 1990

ISBN 0 86267 230 9

This book first appeared as a series of articles in "Recreation Round Up", the official magazine of the Glasgow Telephones Recreation Club, which are reproduced by courtesy of the Editor, Mr. W. J. R. McClure; Assistant Editor, Mr. J. Ashton; Secretary, Mr. A. Brown; and the Executive Committee. Many of the photographs were taken by Mr. R. McMichael and Mr. W. T. M. Rushbury.

contents

The ancient City of Glasgow is rapidly changing its face in what is reported to be the largest redevelopment taking place in Europe. Old landmarks are fast disappearing and towering new architecture, wide sweeping roads and spectacular bridges are taking their place. This is not the first time that Glasgow has led the way in town planning. In 1866 and 1897 the City Improvements Act redeveloped 80 acres around High Street, and many of the well-designed and well-built buildings of that period are still standing today.

A keen desire to write about Glasgow coupled with the encouraging interest of friends prompted me to record the traditions, personalities and worthwhile features of the city before their memory vanished completely from the scene.

A great many people gave me information during my research into the city's history. Everywhere I met with the greatest courtesy and willing co-operation, proving that beneath the surface the Glaswegian is more than ready to talk about the Glasgow of the past of which he is justly proud.

W.W.B.
456 Victoria Road
August 1972   Glasgow

Foreword

IT may seem hard to believe that Glasgow's jostling, bustling street of Trongate was once referred to by Edmund Burke, the Irish writer and statesman, as the finest street in Europe. It may well have been true, however, for Daniel Defoe, the author of "Robinson Crusoe", reiterated this conclusion by stating openly that Glasgow was "the beautifullest little city" he had ever seen.

But Glasgow was then a nutmeg city of 15,000 souls, and the fragrant scented orchards and carefully tended market gardens which were an outstanding feature of the old town were soon to disappear before the advances of a giant building programme which mainly consisted of factories, bridges, railways and warehouses. Industrialisation had arrived — new then, history now.

Let us stroll leisurely along Trongate which was anciently known as St Thenew's Gate, a little path leading to the saint's chapel situated where St Enoch (a corruption of the name) Square is now. Let's be in a receptive mood and learn willingly what the old scene around us had to say.

At 36-38 Trongate we see a brass plaque on the wall commemorating the fact that James Watt had his workshop on this very site "in Buchanansland" in 1763. This plaque like others throughout the city was erected by the 77-strong Pen and

Pencil Club founded in 1877 by writers
and artists who met frequently in the
Royal Tavern, later known as the Royal
Restaurant in West Nile Street.

Many of Watt's most successful exper-
iments were carried out in this workshop,
eventually culminating in the practical
use of steam power which revolutioised
Britain into the industrial age. A few
hours train journey to London today then
took up to 12 days on horseback.

Watt's skill and inventive genius
were rare and versatile. He made and
repaired musical instruments (one of the
organs he built is still on show in the
People's Palace in Glasgow Green) and
became mathematical instrument maker to
the old Glasgow University in High Street.
He directed and supervised the building
of the Monkland Canal to carry coal from
Lanarkshire to the city of Glasgow.

Among the 12 statues in George Square
is one of James Watt erected 13 years
after his death in 1832 at the age of 84.
In spite of his longevity, he had been
delicate and studious as a child and, it
is said, was scolded by his aunt for
wasting time watching the effects of steam
billowing from a kettle spout.

It must be agreed, however, that his
youth did not prove to have been misspent;
with his enterprise and endeavour the
face of the world was changed. In the
following pages we shall see how he and
fellow Glaswegians became involved in the
pages of history...

Trongate

Still in Trongate, it may surprise us to know that this one-time famous and fashionable street was the first in Glasgow to be paved with flagstones. The local people referred to them affectionately as the 'plainstanes'. If you quietly listen and have a receptive ear you may still hear echoes of the footsteps of the 18th century Tobacco Lords as they strutted up and down the plainstanes, proudly dressed in their scarlet coats, curled wigs, cocked hats and carrying gold topped canes, successfully aware of the fact that they had captured half the European tobacco trade imported from their own estates in the American Colonies of Virginia, Carolina and Maryland.

As we approach the Tron church it is interesting to note that many years ago it was razed by fire. The Hell Fire Club broke into the Session House on Valentine's night, plied fuel to the already large fire burning in the fire-

Trongait, 1774

place, in order to find out how much heat they could bear without flinching. The fire got out of control and the resulting conflagration left only the existing steeple as a reminder of the original church.

At No. 90 Trongate and directly above the Bank of Scotland premises, our gaze is attracted to a brass plaque on the wall. The inscription thereon reads: *In a house on this site, Sir John Moore was born on 13th November 1761. He died at Corunna on 16th January 1809.*

Lt. General Sir John Moore, belonged to an illustrious family. His father was a physician and writer of some note, among his works being 'Zeluco' and 'A view of the causes and progress of the French Revolution'. He had been an eye-witness when the mob attacked the Palace of the Tuilleries, wiping out the Swiss Guard and capturing the French King. He founded the Hodge-Podge Club, a literary and debating society which came into being during the affluent period of the Tobacco Lords. It is interesting to note that the cost of a particularly sumptuous meal in the Club's rooms cost 8d. per person. Alas that was 200 years ago.

Doctor Moore knew Robert Burns and had an early and enthusiastic appreciation of his work. Burns sent to him the now historic story of his own life.

Sir John Moore's brother, Admiral Sir Graham Moore also attained fame. During the course of his duties, he engaged four Spanish frigates near Cadiz. They were transporting treasure to the French and with an equal force he captured three vessels and blew up the fourth. The treasure was valued at $3\frac{1}{2}$ million dollars.

Another younger brother, James Carrick Moore, became a surgeon and writer of some note and lived to the ripe age of 98. His daughter lived for over a century.

On his mother's side, Moore was descended from the famous Provost Anderson of Dovehill, who gave his name to the district of Anderson which is now undergoing such a building transformation. Moore fell heir to a third of the estate which was situated approximately where the Goods Station now stands.

Sir John lived the first 11 years of his life in Glasgow and from this point his life blossomed out unexpectedly and certain incidents were instrumental in determining his future military career. His father, the physician, was also tutor to Douglas, the eighth Duke of Hamilton, and accompanied him on a five year tour of the Continent, visiting many countries and studying their languages diligently. During his travels he was well received at the Prussian court and had the opportunity to witness the army tactics of 40,000 troops operating bef re the renowned Frederick II. The military emotions of the young man were strongly excited and one of his first assignments was to go to North America with a punitive force consisting of six companies of the Hamilton Regiment, maintained from the private purse of the Duke.

The American colonists objected to paying taxes to Great Britain which resulted in the actions of an angry mob forcibly boarding a British ship loaded with tea in Boston Harbour and dumping the cargo overside, hence the term, the Boston Tea Party. Independence was granted shortly afterwards and George Washington became the first President of the United States of America.

Twelve years later, Moore was appointed Governor of St. Lucia, one of the Windward Islands where his first task was the crushing of a slave revolt. His troops suffered terribly from conditions and disease and their strength was reduced from 915 to 74 men.

In 1790 he served in the Mediterranean Island of Corsica with notable success and consequently the island came under British rule for two years. During his stay he visited Ajaccio the capital and birthplace of Napoleon. One wonders if the fortunes of war had been slightly loaded in Britain's favour, Napoleon Bonaparte might well have been a corporal in the British Army. At this stage of the war he was in contact with Nelson at Calais, who was commanding a Naval Brigade.

He saw service in such climatically diverse places as Ireland, Sicily, Gibraltar and Sweden as well as Majorca, the pin-up of modern travel brochures.

The campaign for which Moore is best remembered was in Spain. At this period the British Government felt compelled to assist Portugal and Spain to prosecute the war against the French under Napoleon, who sought to deprive the people in these countries of their land and possessions. In the year 1808 he was entrusted with the command of 35,000 troops to aid the Spanish armies and to stem the advance of the French in the Iberian Peninsula. Marshall Soult, the confidant and favourite of Napoleon, with a force of 100,000 men, was endeavouring to cut off the advance of Moore at Salamanca. Moore decided on a tactical withdrawal for 250 miles through wild and desolate country. The troops suffered but he arrived at Corunna still well equipped. But the vagaries of war were present and Moore was chagrined to find that the ships he had ordered to embark his troops from Corunna had not arrived. It transpired that the Dragoon entrusted with the message to the Admiral of the Fleet had fallen in his duty and the message was never delivered.

Moore realised that the situation was critical and decided to cease his retreat. He had many fine troops including the Royal Scots, the oldest regiment in his service and, who became known as 'Pontius Pilate s Bodyguard'. Also present was the Black Watch who had blasted the enemy at Aboukir in Egypt.

The French attacked and the British at first gave way to the weight of numbers and then counter attacked. They thoroughly defeated the French. During the battle Moore was severely wounded and died as victory was assured.

The Rev. Charles Wolfe of Blackhall, County Kildare, Ireland, wrote the 'Burial of Sir John Moore', which reflects on the sad and stirring moment.

Marshall Soult caused a monument to be erected over the grave and the House of Commons gave leave for a monument in St. Paul's Cathedral. So also did the citizens of Glasgow erect a monument to their illustrious son, which was the first of many, in George Square. The Glasgow statue is made from melted down brass cannon on a pedestal of Aberdeen granite. Combined, the weight is 13 tons and with the effigy facing due South,

John Moore statue

down Miller Street, it would appear that John Moore still searches towards the Continent of Europe, perhaps looking for Corunna.

Moore was also M.P. for the burghs of Linlithgow, Selkirk, Lanark and Peebles and in recognition for his services at the Battle of Alexandria, he was awarded the Order of the Bath.

Until six years ago, Moore's cocked hat and sword were on exhibition in the People's Palace, Glasgow Green. They were owned by a descendant residing in a Glasgow Eventide Home who had loaned them to the Corporation. Eventually it was found necessary to sell them at Sotheby's Auction Rooms in London. They were sold for £140 and as the Glasgow Corporation's highest bid was £100, the relics were lost to the City.

Shawfield Mansion

Leaving Sir John Moore's memorial plaque we proceed west-wards along Trongate to the junction of Glassford Street where, on The Commercial Bank of Scotland wall, appears the following:—

> ON THIS SITE
>
> STOOD THE SHAWFIELD MANSION
>
> PRINCE CHARLES STUART
>
> RESIDED IN 1745
>
> Erected by the Pen and Pencil Club
> 1910

The elegant and fashionable Shawfield Mansion, now demolished and its memory descended into the shadows of time, was without doubt the most imposing dwelling in Glasgow and in the days of the affluent epoch of the tobacco lords its prestige was without parallel.

During the turbulent times of the early eighteenth century the house was constructed by Daniel Campbell of Shawfield, Glasgow, Member of Parliament who during his office made himself disliked with the people of Glasgow because of his favour towards the unpopular tobacco tax. Latterly they were further antagonised and riled to the point of rebellion when he voted in agreement with the malt tax which imposed a levy of 3d. on every barrel of beer brewed in Scotland. Particularly in Glasgow, the citizens vigorously opposed the collection of this duty and con-sequently riots flared up and large crowds took control of the city, forcibly preventing the excise officers from collecting the taxes. In this belligerent mood they marched to the Shawfield

Mansion, completely destroying the interior and all the trappings and furnishings. Indeed the m litary had to be called upon to restore peace and order and during the clash many people were killed.

The outcome of this tumult was the arrest of the Provost and Magistrates who were taken as prisoners to Edinburgh and charged with being responsible for the rioting Glaswegians, the deaths of several fellow citizens, putting his Majesty's troops in jeopardy and the wilful destruction of the Shawfield Mansion.

Mr. Daniel Campbell was able to dry his tears with a gilt edged handkerchief however. Parliament approved and commanded that he receive the sum of £9,000 to make up for the loss of his house. Later he purchased the inner Hebridean island of Islay and the money paid in compensation by the town of Glasgow formed a major part of the price paid for it.

Glassford Street, 1820s

In 1760 John Glassford, owner of the Dougalston Estate in Milngavie, bought Shawfield Manison complete with 3½ acres of gard n abundantly provided with varieties of fruit trees and shrubs and laid out to perfection. Its northern boundary touched Ingram Street. Glassford Street, which perpetuates his name, was built approximately on this property.

In the annals of the industrial and commercial history of Glasgow no one played a greater part in the furthering of trade than John Glassford. He owned large and extensive business enterprises in America and in one peak year he imported 4,506 hogsheads of tobacco. His annual turnover was half a million pounds, no small sum in those days. Indeed many of his business books are still kept in the Congress Library in Washington, U.S.A. A fine oil painting of himself and his wife and family hangs on the wall in the Peoples Palace, Glasgow Green. This Virginia Don (Tobacco Lord) died in 1783 and his mortal remains lie buried in the southwest corner of Ramshorn churchyard with this fitting epitaph:—"He who has seen the sunrise and the dawn of the tobacco trade from start to finish".

Across the road from the Shawfield Mansion stood the West Port Well which provided the whole district with its supply of fresh water. Crowds of local women, in pursuit of their domestic duties, went to the well not only for water but to congregate and exchange news with their friends. Very frequently traffic congestion resulted and conditions were further aggravated by some women using the well for washing purposes. Finally the well was dismantled and a not so adequate iron pump substituted. In the eighteenth century Glasgow had approximately 30 wells. Due to the rapid expansion of industrialization and the following growth in population water was, needless to say, becoming an increasingly needed commodity. William Harley, a Glasgow business venture was such a raging success that he is said to have cleared £4,000 annually from it. He was also the first person to construct and provide public baths which were also situated in Bath Street, hence the origin of the name.

But let us go back to Shawfield Mansion and have a look at its most illustrious visitor. Prince Charles Edward Stuart marched into Glasgow at the head of his troops on Christmas Day via the Trongate and stayed for eight days, no doubt glad to be back among their ain folk after a strenuous and exciting march of 580 miles into England. He immediately took over the imposing Shawfield Mansion as his headquarters and it is possible during his stay here that he made the acquaintance of Clementina Walkinshaw, the youngest of the ten daughters of John Walkinshaw of Camlachie and Barrowfield. It was two months since the clansmen had plunged into the hazardous journey into England and their clothes and brogues were badly worn. Glasgow was asked to provide 6,000 pairs of shoes, 6,000 pairs of tartan hose, 6,000 each of short coats and bonnets, 1,200 shirts and a considerable sum of money. Whilst in Glasgow the Prince held two or three parades through the streets and his final parade was on the 2nd of January when the entire army had its first general inspection and review for months. They marched to the selected place with all the indications of a victorious army. A grand sight, shaven and shorn, with pipers playing at the head of the columns, claymores flashing and gleaming. The whole show being enlivened by the bright tartans worn by the respective ely proud of

Water Cart, 1852

manufacturer, shrewdly and intelligently forecast the need and without losing much time laid pipes to carry fresh **water from** springs in his property at Willowbank to a prepared **reservoir** situated where the Corporation Transport Offices now stand in Bath Street. He carried the water around the streets, alleys and closes of Glasgow, selling it to the people at ½d. a stoup and his

clans marching forward as an invincible army intens...
its military achievements. The next day they marched out of
Glasgow in two separate columns, one making its way through
Kilsyth with the Prince at its head and the other via Cumbernauld
with Lord George Murray in command. Sixty recruits raised in
Glasgow marched briskly in their ranks.

Ghosts of Glasgow

From Marland House, which was built adjacent to a site originally known as the Holy Land—a name acquired mainly because of the number of clergy who had taken up residence in this area during its palmy days—we travel eastwards along George Street. This street was opened in 1792 and named after George III and by ordinary standards is not a long street but many famous people were born here or in very close proximity. John A. MacDonald, first Prime Minister of Canada, who has a plaque to his honour in the Ramshorn Church; Sir George Burns, founder of the Cunard Line; Colin Campbell (Lord Clyde) a soldier who participated in the relief of Lucknow; Thomas Campbell, the poet, who composed "Ye Mariners of England" and "Lord Ullin's Daughter"; and William Miller, author of the nursery rhyme "Wee Willie Winkie". It should also be mentioned that Lord Lister, the inventor of antiseptics, had a workshop near the premises of the late Guy Aldred's now demolished Strickland Press. Stopping at the traffic lights at High Street, the ever-changing red, amber and green gives us no indication that this was the site of the historic battle "Bell o' the Brae". Sir William Wallace, in command of 300 chosen cavalry, rode into Glasgow from the town of Ayr on a mission to expel the English from the remainder of the Scottish strongholds. Glasgow Castle or Bishops Palace, which was on the site of the Royal Infirmary and now marked by an obelisk, was garrisoned by 1,000 soldiers under Percy of Northumberland, who held it for the English King. A terrific battle was fought in the narrow streets and alleys of this Cathedral town. Wallace cleft Percy's skull with his mighty sword and many of the fallen leader's troops were slain and the remainder completely routed, never stopping until they reached the safety of Bothwell Castle which was still in their hands. Three hundred and sixty years later, in 1568, Regent Moray, half brother of Mary Queen of Scots, marched through here at the head of his army with 600 Glasgow recruits in its ranks and ultimately shared in the victory at the Battle of Langside.

Away back in the old days many notable people came to Glasgow. Mary Queen of Scots visited Lord Darnley when he was lodging in a house thought to be situated in Rottenrow near the Cathedral. She stayed a week before returning to Edinburgh with her sick husband, who was recovering from smallpox and who was later killed in a controversial gun-powder plot at Kirk o' fields, Edinburgh. Their son was the future King of Great Britain.

Oliver Cromwell stayed in the Saltmarket for a period as did King James VII when he was Duke of York. General Wolfe, of the Siege of Quebec fame, was stationed with his regiment in the infantry barracks. During the Jacobite Rebellion it is interesting to note that these barracks were built on land formerly known as the Butts, where archery was practised diligently by the citizens of Glasgow. The Battle of the Butts was fought here and many hundreds were slain. Barrack Street which perpetuates the name, forms the original boundary of the barracks.

From this traffic lights vantage point, Ladywell Housing Scheme is easily seen. Its elegant lines rise from the gloomy foundations of Duke Street prison where many executions took place and the bodies of criminals lie buried within the precincts. There is little to remind us of this grim place of correction except for the surrounding stone wall which has been preserved, although reduced in height, to maintain a pattern of conformity with the surrounding tenements.

The Molendinar & Cathedral.

Slightly to the east flows Glasgow's sacred river, the Molendinar, where St. Mungo baptised many of his converts in its pristine waters. He lived a simple life in a rough stone cell nearby. From this site rose Glasgow Cathderal, ever zealous of spreading learning and Christianity throughout the country and existing to this day as one of the four pre-Reformation Cathedrals in Scotland still in service as a place of worship. The source of the Molendinar is Hogganfield Loch. Now spurned and rejected, it has been covered up by tarmac only appearing briefly at the city side of the Great Eastern Hotel. Acting as a sewer, it shortly plunges into a dark tunnel to be seen no more until joining the River Clyde. As Glasgow extended and grew in importance, the Molendinar formed a partnership with the Clyde, giving rise to the saying—"Glasgow made the Clyde and the Clyde made Glasgow".

Marland House was built astride Deanside Lane and in the centre of this lane was situated Deanside Well. The Bishop of Glasgow granted this water to the Greyfriars Monastery which was situated where the recently demolished Greyfriars Church stood in North Albion Street. Its water was reputed to be excellent for making punch. King Edward 1st of England is thought to have stayed in this monastery for a period of three days in the Autumn of 1301 and during his visit he made offerings to the shrine of St. Mungo in Glasgow Cathedral.

The Clyde and its tributaries were alive with salmon, so much so that, for the local apprentices, it became a monotonous fare and a stipulation was made in their rules that they did not get salmon more than three times a week. Saltmarket, as the name

Salmon fishing at Govan

indicates, was the place where salt was sold to cure salmon. Perhaps if purification of the rivers ever comes to pass, the salmon may yet return to their ancient spawning grounds. How musical the sound of some of the old Glasgow street names. Spoutmouth, Goosedubs, Schipka Pass, Fiddlers Close, Clayslaps and Candleriggs.

Crossing High Street we enter Duke Street, the longest street in Britain, which was named after the Duke of Montrose and opened in 1794. There we observe a memorial plaque, almost opposite Burrels Lane, situated on the goods station wall and which marks the site of a tenement, previously 36 Duke Street, in which Sam Bough resided in 1850. Sam Bough, landscape painter, was born at Carlisle on the 8th January, 1822. Of humble parentage, he abandoned the prospects of a future in law and followed his natural bent sketching and painting water-colours. Travelling extensively around the country and mixing freely with gipsies, he never attended a school of art but became a member of the Royal Scottish Academy, which exhibited many of his paintings. Bough came to Glasgow from Manchester in 1848 and quickly gained employment as a scene painter in the newly built Princess Theatre, now known as the Citizens Theatre. He furnished landscape sketches for various book publishers including Blackie and Co. Bough lived uncon-ventionally, following the Bohemian life. As a boy he enjoyed the rough-and-tumble sports. He stayed away from home three weeks sketching pictures as fancy led him. While sketching in his native Cumberland, near Rydal, he had the honour to meet Wordsworth the poet. The poet presented him with a copy of his poetic works which were neatly inscribed on the fly-leaf by the donor.

He sketched fifteen pictures in fourteen days in the Anstruther area and he received £750 for a picture entitled "St. Monance—Day after the Storm". Two of his splendid pictures hang in the Peoples Palace, Glasgow Green. They are "The Glasgow Bridge" and the "Victoria Bridge" which portray a wealth of detail and high-light the artist's versatile skill. In April 1849 he married a Miss Elizabeth Taylor, a leading contralto in the St. Andrews Church, which is the oldest Episcopalian Church, since the Reformation, in Scotland and the marriage certificate can still be seen in the church register. This church is also the oldest church in Glasgow with the exception of Glasgow Cathedral. Unfortunately it may be in the path of the Ring Road and its future as a place of worship, or at least an ancient monu-ment, is in question. General Wolfe worshipped here in 1753 when he was stationed at the barracks and while serving under the Duke of Cumberland. This church having no precenter, was known as the Whistling Kirk because it had an organ or a "kist of whistles". Those who are interested should certainly take the opportunity now of viewing the interior of this beautiful church with its many interesting exhibits.

Ramshorn Church

Passing the Ramshorn Church in Ingram Street, Glasgow, anyone who was moved to linger awhile and reflect on the serenity and historical aspects of this early 19th century structure, might well imagine that nothing had ever disturbed the peace and quiet of this apparently hallowed place except, perhaps, for the birds who sing sweetly in the leafy branches of the churchyard trees, wheeling and flitting over the scattered tombstones which indicate the last resting place of many former worthies of the city.

That little flock of the feathered creatures, preening themselves on the wall overlooking the grave of Pierre Emile Langelier, may call to mind that over a hundred years ago Glasgow was the

Old Ramshorn Church

central point of a sensational world-wide murder trial, when Madeleine Smith was accused of murdering Pierre, a humble clerk from the Channel Islands. His name is not on the tomb-stone, but there is an entry in the record of burials, which can be found in the Mitchell Library. It simply states:—

"To Pierre Emile Langelier, clerk, sudden death. Lair holder, James Fleming, 5 E.M."

These birds, rising in a graceful arc from the grassy verge have just left their perch beside the resting place of William Glen, the author of "*Wae's me for Prince Charlie*," well-known Jacobite song.

Twittering loudly, they alight daintily on the square-topped tower and, with cocky eye, look down on Ingram Street. Here, due to the extension of the road, which necessitated covering a part of the graveyard, the pedestrians now walk over the initialled graves of the Foulis Brothers, who were the publishers of the *Glasgow Courant*, forerunner of the *Glasgow Herald*, an early Glasgow paper, which was one of those which gave a first-hand account of the Battle of Culloden, news then, memories now.

In the period of time which heralded the dawn of the industrial revolution, the spacious orchards crowded the boundary walls of the church, but later they were cut down to make way for multi-storied office blocks and workshops, which now leer down at her smoke-covered walls, and the broken tombstones, their once sharply-cut epitaphs scarcely readable now. Jealously, the old church guards its story.

A strange practice was at one time carried out by the students of Glasgow University, under the leadership of a bold Glasgow youth called Mr. Granville Sharp Pattison. When their exploits were made public, the revelation filled the people with horror and revulsion at the grim news that many students had become resurrectionists.

Such was the zeal and desire of these students for the fur-therance of their calling in the medical and surgical fields, that they drew lots in the quiet secrecy of their retreat. The selected students were automatically nominated to rob one of the graves which might prove to be of interest, in one of the surrounding churchyards.

Ramshorn Churchyard was situated in close proximity to their quarters, consequently the graves in it were frequently raided under cover of darkness, and the silent burden, carried away in a sack, would add another subject to their anatomy table for analysis and diagnosing.

Indeed, body-snatching became so profitable that many unscrupulous men participated in this gruesome trade, supplying bodies which had only recently been interred, to fulfil the doctors' demands. High prices were paid, ranging from £5 to £20 and £30, depending on the requirements of the dissecting table. These were no small sums in these days, when many honest folk were working for only 3d. a day.

These events caused the city to be in an uproar, so that a reign of terror started and, to counteract the desecretion of graves, the adult, fit population had to take turns at patrolling the church precincts. Matters came to a climax when the students robbed

Glasgow Medical Students

the grave of a famed local beauty, a Mrs. McAlister, wife of a well-known haberdasher in Hutcheson Street, Glasgow.

A brother of the deceased noticed that the grave had been disturbed and, on closer examination, it was found that the body had been removed.

An enraged mob attacked the University in High Street, smashing windows and creating general havoc, and after a thorough search by some of the town's leading officials, parts of bodies were discovered, including among them that of Mrs. McAlister.

Mr. Granville Sharp Pattison and his fellow students were tried in Edinburgh, but were acquitted. However, the feelings of the people were so incensed against the desecrator that he had to go to America, where he became an eminent surgeon and physician.

But still the story of Ramshorn Church goes on. A plaque was unveiled in recent years within the church walls to commemorate Sir John McDonald, the first Prime Minister of Canada, who was reputed to have been born in the district.

She still holds her place as a venerated place of worship, although it is a far cry from the era when her doors were opened for the first time in a nutmeg city of a few thousand population.

St. David's Church, erected on Ramshorn site in 1824

Ramshorn Church boasts what may be said to be the finest collection of stained glass windows in the country. The sunbeams shining strongly through the multi-coloured Biblical characters shows the quality of stained glass at its very best. They were an extremely popular exhibit when on view to the public at the end of last century.

Further, a mort-safe which lay rusting away in the church-yard has been gifted to the People's Palace where it can be seen now. It is a heavy iron erection which was placed over the grave to defeat the attention of the body snatchers.

High Street

We are now in High Street which was opened in the year 1100 and so named because it led to the highest part of the town. It immediately gained importance when the University was built on it's East side in 1460. In 1750 Glasgow boasted the possession of 13 streets but since then it has stretched out its ever-reaching tentacles and casually embraced towns, villages and spacious country regions into its commercial bosom and forming the network into a vast, vibrating, vital city. The countryside taken over has been transformed in so many ways that where once the Peeswit and the Whaup flew and sang in undisturbed silence, the roaring traffic and rushing tumult has taken precedence.

College & High Street, 1800's

Soon we arrive at Nicholas Street, unpretentious to the eye, but it's name bristles with legend and romance. It was known, in the latter part of the last century, as Greyfriars Wynd because it led to the Greyfriars Monastery which stood on the site of the Greyfriars Church in Albion Street and which was recently demolished. Originally there was a saint Nicholas Street running adjacent to St. Nicholas Hospital, also known as The Provand's Lordship (the oldest house in Glasgow and founded in 1471 by Bishop Muirhead) which is situated opposite Cathedral Square.

St. Nicholas is the Patron Saint of Russia and also of children, seafarers and merchants. The name gradually evolved into Santa Claus and as is well known, the spirit of Santa Claus still manifests itself each year by the tradition of giving gifts.

Pope Nicholas V who was borne in 1398 at Pisa, Italy, granted a papal edict for the erection of the first Glasgow university in 1451 which was duly built and stood for nine years at the North side of Rottenrow, before being transferred and rebuilt in High Street. There was also a Bishop of Glasgow named Nicholas de Moffat, so this humble, dejected Nicholas Street, which we are now surveying, has very strong ecclesiastical connections indeed.

We observe with interest, chiselled on the corner of the British Linen Bank buildings in Nicholas Street, a sculptured picture of a large, gabled house and figures of people dressed tastefully in clothes of the George IV period. These are deftly cut in the red sandstone and on it the lettering briefly states that ON THIS SITE STOOD THE HOUSE IN WHICH POET CAMPBELL LIVED.

On further examination of this bank building we see that it is a finely constructure of a rare architectural design complete with the full sized statue of a man or woman and situated in a commanding position high at the top of the edifice. In a brief glance we might imagine this figure to represent Santa Claus or even Thomas Campbell, but according to the British Linen Bank authorities it is thought to be Pallas, the Goddess of Wisdom and Weaving, pertaining to Greek mythology and is the symbol depicted on their current Bank seal.

Thomas Campbell, poet, was born on 27th July 1777. He was the youngest of a family of eleven and his Father and Mother were both named Campbell although not related by blood. Their respective family trees branched and spread back to the same district in Argyll and his father was engaged in the lucrative tobacco trade.

He entered Glasgow University at the early age of 12 and was eventually elected Lord Rector on three successive occasions in 1826-1828. It is interesting to note that Sir Walter Scott also stood for election at this period.

Campbell was the author of the poem ' Pleasures of Hope ' and his favourite stamping ground for inspiration while composing those world wide, applauded verses, was the vicinity of Arthur's Seat in Edinburgh, where he was staying at the time. It was the year 1799 and he was 21 years of age. Much of the phraseology and delightful words of this poem have been serviced into everyday speech. For the first edition of ' Pleasures of Hope ' he received the sum of £60. About this period of time, Lord Byron, Wordsworth and Sir Walter Scott were also competing in the literary market.

" COMING EVENTS CAST THEIR SHADOWS BEFORE ". It took poet Campbell an entire week of labourious study to cast this phrase to his satisfaction. He travelled extensively and many of his finest poems and lyrics were inspired and composed in places far from his home town. While acting in the capacity of tutor in the Island of Mull, he composed " Gertrude of Wyoming " (considered the gem of all his poems) featuring American life, although he had never been in America.

His imagination was fired and stimulated by the fairy-like scenery seen when looking over the Sound of Jura as well as providing the basis which shaped the characters in his poems " Lord Ullin's Daughter " and " Glenara ".

He composed the stirring poem "Hohenlinden" and gained first hand facts of the battle while watching the struggle between the victorious French and the Austrians, from the quiet retreat and vantage point of St. James' Monastery in Bavaria. While staying in Altona, near Hamburg, Germany, he compiled the verses, "Ye Mariners of England".

He visited Paris in 1814 and met Wellington, the conquerer of Bonaparte at Waterloo, Baron von Humboldt, the German scientist and Madam de Stael, the French writer who wrote " Corrine " and which is acclaimed throughout Europe as an outstanding work.

He was deeply impressed by the works of art in the Louvre, of which many priceless collections were gathered by Napoleon during his campaigns in Europe. He visited Algiers in 1832 where he wrote " Letters from the South ", a titillating and knowledgeable account of his travels, in two volumes. He is also given credit as the originator and instigator of the founding of the London University in 1825.

In his later years he spent much of his time in London, but when a boy, he enjoyed several vacations in nearby Cathcart, around 1818, amid the pleasant, green, rolling countryside of that period. This episode was stamped indelibly in his mind as the following lines show and which he wrote during a much later visitation.

Scenes of my childhood and dear to my heart,
Ye green, waving woods, on the banks of the Cart,
How oft in the morning of life I have strayed
By the stream of the vale and the grass covered glade.
Then then every rapture was young and sincere
ere the sunshine of life had been stained by a tear.

I might add the information that the foregoing lines are not very widely known to the public.

He took a great interest in the struggles of Poland and Greece who were struggling for their independence and fittingly enough, a guard of Polish exiles marched with his cortege when the funeral procession passed on its way to Westminster Abbey and finally to Poet's Corner, where he was laid to rest with the due reverence beside Addison, Goldsmith and Sheridan. A Polish nobleman threw a handful of earth, collected from the tomb of Kosciusko (famous leader of Poland) and scattered it on the grave.

There is a monument erected to the memory of Thomas Campbell in George Square, situated opposite the Head Post Office and the inscription simply states: —

THOMAS CAMPBELL
Poet
Born 1777   Died 1844
By J. Mossman H.R.S.A.

This monument was unveiled in 1877, the centenary of his birth.

Old College

If we proceed down High Street,
we will notice a plaque situated on the south end of the College
Goods Station Railway Office building on which is written:—

ON THIS SITE STOOD THE UNIVERSITY OF GLASGOW

FROM 1460 TILL 1870.

THE MAIN GATEWAY, NOW RE-ERECTED AT GILMOREHILL,

WAS OPPOSITE COLLEGE STREET.

With this information arousing our curiosity and anxious to
learn more, we continue our journey and in a few steps reach the
site stated, opposite College Street. The information is certainly
correct for the place is marked by a large memorial stone set into
the wall of the VISTA VENETIAN BLINDS office building (at
one time the premises of Alston's Tea Rooms). The coat of arms
of the University is colourfully displayed on the upper portion of
the stone and was recorded by the Glasgow University in the year
1900.

In the year 1888, Sir William Pearce, Bart., the well-known
shipbuilder, paid for the removal and re-erection of the Gateway
to its present position at the North Eastern entrance, University
Avenue, Gilmorehill, and it is now known as Pearce Lodge.

Indeed, if we move to the nearby entrance to the Goods
Station and look through the closed Ironwork gateway, the scene
before us presents a complete state of decay and dereliction. Miles
of rails have been uplifted and the death knell has rung for the
freight trains, which until recently, clanged their way, noisily, into
the station. There is a ghost-like atmosphere pervading the yard,
which is reputed to have been the largest in the world in days
gone by.

The adjacent portion, called High Street Goods Station, was
known as College Station until 1907 and at this period it was
re-modelled and became known as High Street Station. This section
still functions freely and something like the old bustle still prevails.

Overall, however, the picture portrayed is a mixture of decline and fall.

It may stagger the imagination if one tries to visualise that over 100 years ago this area was a scene of beauty and elegance. Within these boundaries stood the stately buildings of the University, the splendid Hunterian Museum, the beautifully designed Blackfriars Church, the wealthily endowed Blackfriars' Monastery, a conservatory and the historic Infantry Barracks. It may lend to a clearer picture if these places are described separately.

Firstly, the old University stood on this site for 400 years until its removal to Gilmorehill in 1870. Adjacent was the College Green, the recreational and fresh air lung of the University, and

Old College, 1692

which stretched to the East as far as Hunter Street. It was tastefully studded with trees with the sacred Molendinar flowing through the green's spacious lawns, sweeping past the observatory and its well tended gardens on its way to the River Clyde.

The Hunterian Museum was considered one of the finest edifices in Glasgow and was gifted by Dr. William Hunter, one of the famous Hunter brothers who were born in Long Calderwood, East Kilbride. At the time of its transfer to a special wing built in Gilmorehill in 1873, the exhibits were considered to be the finest collection in Europe and valued at £65,000. It had a library of 12,000 volumes and is still open for public viewing.

Blackfriars Church, considered by Milne, the architect to Charles I, to surpass in design and beauty almost any church in Scotland, was rendered unserviceable when it was struck by lightning in 1668, but was rebuilt and re-named College Church.

The Blackfriars Monastery was in line with Blackfriars Street which perpetuates the name of this wealthy institution. The prefix was adopted because the monks wore black habits and hoods and it was the only sanctuary in the West of Scotland where refugees and law breakers could seek shelter and protection beyond the reach of the law.

The Infantry Barracks were situated between Hunter Street and Barrack Street on the site of the ancient Butts where the citizens practised archery, scoring marks at the popinjay. Incidentally, there is a tavern in the Stockwell called The Popinjay.

In 1301, Edward I of England worshipped at the Blackfriars Church, during a campaign in Scotland. His army, comprising 7,000 foot and 500 cavalry were probably stationed in an encampment on the Gallowmuir where the Butts and Barracks were latterly built.

Alas, when the Railway bought this ground all these fine buildings were swept away including many churches and schools in Bell Street and Duke Street. According to M'Ilwraith the historian, the opening up of this extremely congested part of the city, with houses of poor sanitary conditions, ill lit and badly ventilated, dirty and swarming with the lowest classes of the community, there has been a new lung added to the locality in a wide space, clear of buildings of any kind. But one wonders why the original fresh air lung of the University grounds was substituted for the smoke-filled lung of the railway yards.

Be that as it may, without doubt there were many outstanding buildings cleared away with the slums to make way for the railway. Havannah Street, which was in line with Nicholas Street was engulfed by the Goods Station extension. It had been opened in 1763 and named to commemorate the capture of the capital of Cuba.

The remains of the old College Churchyard had to be removed to the Craigton Cemetery and the Central Necropolis, under the supervision of the city's Sanitary Department. In the joint Craigton and Cardonald Cemetery offices in Mosspark Boulevard, the burial records for the year 1876 show the entries, marked in red, of the re-interments from the College Churchyard. Some of the remains have possibly been buried for hundreds of years and all identities have been lost and, apparently, there are no tombstones marking their new resting places in Craigton. However, layer F. 515 was discovered in the South West corner at the rear of Moss Heights and proved to be a beautiful, unpolished, granite column to Dr. Cleghorn of Shawfield, a one time lecturer in chemistry at the University in the High Street. He was the first physician-in-charge appointed to the first asylum for lunatics opened in Parliamentary Road in 1814. He had a portrait painted by the famous Sir Henry Raeburn which now hangs in Gartnavel Hospital and he was succeeded by Dr. Balmanno, whose mother had a physic garden in Balmano Street, now swallowed up by our own Head-quarters, Marland House. He also had a portrait of himself, by Raeburn.

Dr. Cleghorn's tombstone is marked by his wife's name Thomson and the information of the re-interment is briefly advised on the stone.

John, the 3rd Earl of Lennox, sold the fertile lands of Cowglen, Hillfield, Arden, Deaconsbank, and Patterton to George, son of Sir John Maxwell of Netherpollok in 1518. He also had, as residences, the Palace of Inchinnan, Crookston Castle and Dumbarton Castle. He was assassinated by James Hamilton of Finnart at Manuel outside Stirling while attempting to save the life of James V, in the year 1526. His burial took place in Blackfriars Monastery which was also the last resting place of many of the local lairds, including the Stewarts, Lords of Castlemilk, the ancient lands which have been taken over as a Glasgow Housing Estate.

Lord Darnley, who married Mary, Queen of Scots, was of the same ilk as John III, Earl of Lennox.

Perhaps the occupant of some forgotten grave has been overlooked during the re-interments and still lies in his earthy bed. Perhaps also, disturbed and restless beneath the vast network of Railway lines, having to endure a Dante's inferno for well nigh a hundred years with only the everlasting grinding of engine wheels and the rhythmic roar of the piston rods, his only lullaby.

The well known Lion and Unicorn staircase which was a feature of the old university is one of the few reminders in stone that has been re-erected at Gilmorehill. It is adorned tastefully with a unicorn on the right and a lion on the left, the heraldic figures signifying the honour of Scotland.

Lion and Unicorn Staircase, Old College

The day before the university was taken over by the Railway Authorities, the professors were photographed, standing on the staircase.

The Blackstone Chair is a traditional piece of furniture transferred to Gilmorehill as a worthy memento of the old university. The students passed their examinations seated in this chair. Its component parts are a slab of black marble, a framework of dark oak and attached to the back of the chair an hour glass, its purpose to register exactly the length of the examination. The back of the chair is ornately carved, the upper part depicting the Royal Arms of Scotland and the lower part, the Royal Arms of England.

It may be difficult to realise that the College Yard was once the rallying ground for Highland Games. The London Illustrated News of August, 1867, contained a photograph of the games. It shows the fine buildings, the green lawns and the kilted figures taking part in all the activities of a full fledged sporting arena. This period was 13 years prior to the university being moved to its new building.

When the Railways took over the university lands the buildings were all swept away and the stones promptly used to construct station foundations and for levelling-off purposes.

Beneath the level of the station yards are built a vast labyrinth of vaults that afford splendid storage space. Fruitbrokers, L. H. Williams and Ratcliffe & Shearer at 138 and 140 High Street, utilise the vaults for storing fruit.

In Duke Street, Glasgow Bonding Company store whisky in the spacious vaults that spread well under the surface of the station. Bell Street also has vaults which Arbuckle, Smith & Co. use for storage of merchandise. A large warehouse nearby is used by the Railway Bonding Co. for storage of whisky and it is said that the total value of this whisky stored hereabouts is possibly £4 million when exported abroad.

If one were privileged to walk through the extensive policies of the Goods Yards an amazing scene would meet the eye. Before us lie a great number of railroads branching and spreading off into various sheds. An interesting point was brought to light when an official pointed out that one of these "roads" was called the Liffey Road. On the day on which this particular length of railway was brought into service, a man by the name of Pasha Liffey was hanged for murder in the nearby Duke Street prison. It has, since then been called the Liffey Railroad in memory of the doomed man.

Pasha Liffey was an itinerant boxer, twenty years of age. He was born in Mafeking, Basutoland, and paid the supreme penalty for murdering a 64-years-old woman, Mary Jane Welsh, wife of a miner at Dykehead Road and belonging to Dykehead Rows, Larkhall.

Precisely at quarter to eight, the prison bell rang out its mournful toll proclaiming to all listeners that the prisoner was on his last walk to the gallows. At one minute past eight the black flag was unfurled and fluttered solemnly from the highest building in the prison. Pierrepont was the executioner, his first visit to Glasgow.

The day the students left the old university, they lighted their torches and in time honoured fashion marched to their new quarters at Gilmorehill.

The country estates of Gilmorehill and Donaldshill were the cradle of the new university. Gilmorehill House was demolished but a painting of it can be seen in the Bellfield Museum, Kilmarnock.

The first graduation ceremony at Gilmorehill was for the Prince of Wales (King Edward VII). He received an honorary degree Doctor of Laws and he laid the foundation stone of the university.

We have a last look at the old university and it occurs to us that the idea of the steam engine had been born within this area and had now taken control of it. But, part of the station has been given back to nature, if only temporarily. Her practised hand has well painted the derelict station with a variety of colourful wild flowers such as fireweed, black nightshade and red poppy and has added brightness to the man-made drabness.

Foulis Academy Exhibition in College Quadrangle, 1761

Victorian Glasgow

Perhaps someone, somewhere, while delving deeply in their garden, or some workman digging a trench, may have the good luck to discover a corner stone and its treasure, intact. A small fortune may await them for there are certain to be some ancient coins, in mint condition and which will fetch a handsome price for the finder.

At the erection of a building, a corner stone was and is usually laid by some notable person. It was the custom to deposit in a cavity in the stone a collection of current coins newspapers and other items of interest, when the stone was carefully sealed up. When the time would eventually arrive for the building to be demolished it is natural that the corner stone would be of particular interest. Unfortunately, corner stones are not always located even after painstaking search by demolishers. Regretfully it is cleared away with the debris and will, no doubt, be used for new road foundations or other such purposes. The corner stone of Greyfriars Church, Albion Street, was never discovered during demolitions. Likewise, the corner stones of the British Linen Bank and adjacent Harrington Building in Ingram Street and Hanover Street, which are in the course of demolition, have so far remained undiscovered.

A great quantity of the stone used to build early Glasgow came from the Giffnock Quarries and some of the large, dressed stone weighed as much as one or two tons (120-130 lbs. to the cubic foot). Draught horses hauled the quarried stones to the building site.

In the City of Glasgow, if one is interested enough to look around the surrounding buildings, there will be surprise at the exquisite architectural design of most of the structures, especially if we but lift our eyes and survey the building from top to bottom, in all its fullness. The splendid workmanship of by-gone days shines through the accumulated dirt and grime of the passing years and even in spite of the unseemly alterations which mar the original design and where the ravages of dilapidation have left their mark, their beauty is still discernable and not totally lost to us.

Most of Glasgow was built in the Victorian era and it is often referred to as a Victorian City. Many outstanding architects have played their part in the construction of these fine buildings which were erected during the rapid expansion of the industrial period of the last century.

We are indebted to such men as Greek Thomson, born 1817, died 1878. He was the seventeenth child of a family of twenty. He designed the 113 years old Caledonia Road Church and it has now been considered worthy of preservation. It is reckoned by experts to be the best example of its type in the world.

Charles Rennie Mackintosh, born 1868, died 1928, was the architect for the much admired School of Art, built in 1907 and situated at 167 Renfrew Street.

Robert Adam, born 1728, died 1792, was the most famous of four brothers namely, James, John and William, all noted architects. He was born in Kirkcaldy.

James was associated with Robert in all his work and he held the eminent position of architect to George III. He was appointed Master Mason of the Board of Ordinance in Scotland. The four brothers were responsible for many important buildings in London, such as Whitehall and the district of Adelphi. Their skill and enterprise greatly improved the architectural features of the Metropolis. Robert Adam was buried in Westminster Abbey.

They also designed furniture in tasteful keeping with their interior decorations and the beauty and elegance of those furnished apartments cannot be surpassed for charm and loveliness, even to the present day. Their work is still high'y valued.

William Adam planned Pollok House, Pollokshaws and this was the only one of his buildings in the vicinity of Glasgow built as long ago as 1752. This fine house is now a museum and the public have free access to view the many exhibits and an opportunity to visit the adjoining gardens.

Many of the fine buildings are fast disappearing in the present redevelopment of the City. Perhaps at this point we could have a look at two edifices of Corinthian style, erected by James Adam in 1793-5, situated on each side of College Street at High Street. They were originally built for the University staff when the University of Glasgow was situated in High Street.

College Street was then the main roadway leading to the chief entrance of the University and still retains the name. The structures have been sadly neglected and badly mutilated by indifferent alterations from time to time. There is evidence, however, that they have been used for purposes other than dwelling houses. On casual observation it will be noticed, high up on the face of the North building faded lettering of words extracted from texts in the Bible which are still visible and seem to indicate that it has been used as a church at some time in the past.

Our eyes continue to search over the once classical South edifice and to our surprise we notice a plaque at 177 High Street, situated at second floor level. It was placed there in memory of William Motherwell and simply states:—

> IN THIS TENEMENT,
> WILLIAM MOTHERWELL, POET,
> WAS BORN 13th OCTOBER 1797.

The poems which Williams Motherwell wrote were drawn largely from the old songs and stories of Scotland and in this respect he can be classified with Sir Walter Scott and the Ettrick Shepherd.

His father was an ironmonger and he removed to Edinburgh with his family and stayed there for a period of 8 years. While attending the school of William Lennie, who wrote the once well known Lennie Grammar, he met a girl who was the same age as himself. Her name was Jeanie Morrison, daughter of an Alloa brewer and she was the inspiration of his best poem which he named after her.

His poem 'My Heid So Like to Rend, Willie' can hardly be equalled in Scottish poetry if only by the strength of its sad pathos. As an example of its tenderness, here is the first stanza:—

> My heid is like to rend Willie,
> My heart is like to break —
> I'm wearing aff my feet, Willie,
> I'm dyin' for your sake!
> Oh lay your cheek to mine Willie,
> Your hand on my breast-bane —

Oh say you'll think on me, Willie,
When I am deid an' gane.

At the age of fifteen he gained a position in the Sheriff's Office in Paisley. He eventually rose to the rank of Sheriff Depute for Renfrewshire.

In 1830 he was the Editor of the Glasgow Courier, one of the City's early newspapers. He was also Editor of the Paisley Advertiser and the Paisley Magazine, and compiled and composed a collection of poems known as Minstrelry Ancient and Modern which were published in Glasgow in 1827 and considered of high repute. In 1819 he was instrumental in the collection of material for "The Harp of Renfrewshire", consisting of songs and essays edited in 1819. According to reports this is, nowadays, a very rare edition indeed.

Motherwell was in contact with Sir Walter Scott and Edgar Allen Poe, the American writer who paid compliment to him in his essay on "The Poetic Principle" which referred to the 'Song of the Cavalier' which Motherwell wrote.

He was a pupil of Paisley Grammar School and he showed great skill in sketching. His handwriting was of such high quality that on a brief glance it could be mistaken for copper plate engraving. He was Secretary of the Paisley Burns Club and in the Club premises was erected a life-sized bust to his memory. It stands, at the present time, in the Sheriff Clerk's Office, James Street, Paisley. Some of his original poems are on view in the Paisley Museum.

He wrote a poem on Crookston Castle which stands within the boundaries of Glasgow and which had appealing and romantic connections with the ill-fated Mary, Queen of Scots and Lord Darnley.

At the age of 37 Motherwell died and was buried in the Central Necropolis on 5th November 1835. His grave is marked by a handsome monument complete with a full sized bust of the likeness of the poet. On the face of the tombstone are clearly depicted a number of martial scenes from passages in his stirring poems.

Over a period of 118 years the sun and storm have had little effect on the tomb but the vandals have been more successful in their efforts, as seen by the shattered stonework. It is stated that the stone was gifted by admirers of his poetic genius and he lies in the little Molendinar Glen in a position almost in line with Glasgow Cathedral.

Perhaps the Necropolis, because of its high altitude can be likened to the impressive Tohmnahurich cemetery, Inverness. The former is 223 feet high, the latter, 181 feet.

If we walk into No. 10 College Street and proceed to the back of the houses, we can still see a fragment of the old Meal Mill Market wall, built of undressed stone and which was in operation in the 17th century. It lay between Shuttle Street and High Street. Shuttle Street acquired its name from the lands of Shuttlefield on which it is built.

Diagonally across the street at 38 to 50 College Street stands a picturesque edifice which was originally built as a Fire Station. At present it provides accommodation for the staffs of the Corporation Highways Department and business firms, J. C. Rennie, Produce Brokers, Fraser, Summers & Faucard, Egg Importers and H. McKenzie, a Locksmith. The building is extremely neglected and it would appear that its days of service are numbered, although the topmost part of the building is still in use for dwelling houses.

College Street Fire Station was brought into use in 1851. In 1900 it was removed to Ingram Street where it still remains. In the early days at College Street many hectic scenes were witnessed when the firemen were suddenly summoned to duty. Before the station acquired horses of its own, they employed 'Carters' and hired horses. The first horse to reach a fire earned ten shillings for the driver. Naturally there was keen competition as the butts (water barrels) careered through the streets to get to their target as quickly as possible.

The story of College Street Fire Station would not be complete if reference was not made to WALLACE, the Fire Dog. He was a stray collie dog which wandered into the station 85 years ago and was befriended by the firemen. When the dog died the taxidermists did their work and the animal can be seen in its glass case in the rest room of the Station, complete with little rubber boots which were made for the dog in its lifetime. Visitors are free to visit the exhibit on request at the fire station enquiry office.

Robert Burns

Burns visited Glasgow and he stayed at the Black Bull Inn. A Scottish Burns Club Tablet, placed on the wall at the corner of Virginia Street and Argyle Street, gives us a brief history:

Robert Burns

Lodged here when this building

was the Black Bull Inn.

He visited Glasgow

June 1787, February and March 1788.

It was while staying in the Black Bull Inn that Burns wrote his love epistle to Clarinda who inspired him to write the beautiful love song "Ae Fond Kiss". Burns does not appear to have had a great many physical ties with Glasgow but some people might

The Black Bull Inn, 1850s

be unaware of the fact that Burns has a daughter buried in the Vennel burying ground at Pollokshaws. She was a Mrs. John Thomson, whose mother was Annie Park, niece of Mrs. Hyslop, of the Globe Hotel, Dumfries. Mrs. Thomson died in 1873 at the ripe old age of 82. Her grave is marked by a long low tombstone with eight verses inscribed thereon which were written by her second son, Robert Burns Thomson. Another Glasgow connection was with John Wilson, a teacher and Session Clerk, who was the prototype of Dr. Hornbrook. The satire Burns composed brought John Wilson publicity and consequently paved the way so that he became fairly prosperous. He is buried in the Old Gorbals Burying Ground at Rutherglen Road, Glasgow.

The Lass O'Ballochmyle was Miss Wilhelmina Alexander who inspired Burns to compose the delightful song of the same name. She lived for a period in a house where the Glasgow Municipal Buildings now stand and died there in 1843 at the age of 88, unmarried. Her burial place is unknown.

Burns visited the Black Bull Inn which was the rendezvous of the elite and fashionable of the city. The Highland Society of Glasgow, which was formed in 1727, purchased the land for £260:11:6 and then built the hotel in 1758. The adjoining stables had accommodation for 38 horses and the hay loft could easily hold 30 tons of hay. The funds to build the hotel were obtained in a novel way. George Whitefield, the famous 18th century evangelist, preached a rousing sermon to a vast crowd in the graveyard of Glasgow Cathedral and, at the suggestion of the Highland Society, he kindly consented to take a special collection, the proceeds being sufficient to build the Black Bull Hotel.

Tobaccoland

Virginia Street was opened in 1753 and named after the American tobacco state of Virginia which brought great trade to the city of Glasgow. Provost Andrew Buchanan of Glasgow, whose family owned the estates of Drumpellier and Mount Vernon, built Virginia Street and also a palatial mansion which was situated in Virginia Street between Ingram Street and Wilson Street. It was demolished in 1840 to make way for the Union Bank and is now known as Lanarkshire House. Virginia Street was a great banking centre in its early days and has the distinction of being one of the oldest banking sites in Great Britain. It housed the Thistle Bank, The Ship Bank, The Union Bank, Thomson's Bank and the City Bank which crashed in 1878, the effects of which had severe repercussions on the commercial life of the City. The Union Bank is possibly one of the oldest Banks in the city.

Magnificent mansions were erected in Virginia Street and the traces of early grandeur can still be seen. At No. 42 is a notable example of a typical tobacco lords mansion. At first glance one is impressed by the elegant architectural design of the facade. The warehouse of Stirlings now occupy the building and if one is privileged to visit the restaurant a notice hanging on the wall will be observed.

At the south corner of Wilson Street and Virgina Street is situated probably one of the oldest buildings in Virginia Street, its cellar containing an ancient Glasgow well. On the opposite side of the street, at No. 33, is the Crown Arcade which was the old tobacco auction rooms, and later was used for auctioning sugar. The interior has two ornately fashioned galleries from which the tobacco lords looked over the goods for sale on display in the hallway below. The place has now been converted into a number of offices.

Virginia Street was built outside the West Port, one of the gates of Glasgow which could readily be shut against unwelcome intrusion. It was the first of many new streets built outside the city barrier. The West port was demolished in 1751.

Glassford Street was opened in 1793 and named after Glassford a tobacco lord who owned Dougalston Estate near Milngavie.

It has been said that, running underground to the Clyde, there exists a smugglers passage leading from the basement of Glen and Davidson Glassford Street. The passage was apparently easy to tunnel when it was constructed in the old days as the tunnellers had only to penetrate through sand. During the last war sand taken from this tunnel was found suitable for filling sand bags.

In the early days of Glasgow all the main roads entering the town were safeguarded by ports or gates and could be shut readily in times of emergency. Customs and dues on merchandise coming into the town were levied at these strategical points.

The earliest five principal gates were situated at the north, south, east, west and at the old stockwell Bridge over the Clyde. The Saracen Head Inn was built in 1755 at the East Port in the

Saracen's Head Courtyard, 1850s

Gallowgate. Complying as the counterpart of the Black Bull Inn situated at the West Port, the Saracen Head Inn was built from stones taken from the ruins of the Bishops Palace which was situated in Cathedral Square in front of the Royal Infirmary. When the nearby East Port near Ross Street was demolished in 1749 the stones from it were also used to help to build the Saracen Head Inn. The Saracen Head Inn was erected on the site of the little St. Mungo's Chapel Kirkyard which was built in the year 1500. In 1600 it was converted and made into a leper hospital.

The Saracen Head Inn in its day was considered the essence of modernity and the management advertised proudly that the beds were all good and clean and free from bugs. The inn was the haunt of the fashionable set and many important functions took place within its walls. The stables of this hostelry could house 60 horses and it was in this hotel, in 1773, that Boswell and Dr. Johnston stayed after their return from a tour in the Hebrides.

At the corner of Saracen Head Lane and Gallowgate there is a public house called the Saracen Head. It occupies the same site as the old Saracen Head Inn which was removed in 1905. The present proprietor of this public house reports that a number of years ago, during digging operations for the foundations of the adjacent Saracen Head Tenement, a number of skeletons were unearthed and were ultimately reinterred in the Necropolis. The proprietor retained four skulls. He had them expertly cleaned and polished and placed three of them on display in the interior of his premises. In a measure this conformed to the tradition of the Saracen Head and the name of his public house. As a memento and souvenir he took the last one home which after skillful examination, proved to be the skull of a young girl of 15 who had died of leprosy many hundreds of years ago. He named the skull Maggie and goes on to say that whenever he felt unduly bumptious or big headed, he looked at Maggie who appeared to return his gaze reproachfully and seemed to say "Be careful man. Remember you are only mortal. Look what's happened to me."

The Saracen Head public house has on show several relics connected with Saracen Head Inn. Among them is a pistol carried for protection on the coach which travelled from London to Saracen Head Inn on its final eight hour stage. Also there is the fireplace which heated the bedroom in which Dr. Johnston slept during his stay.

In the backcourt, at the rear of the Saracen Head Tenement, there is an old well where it is reputed that St. Colomba, who brought christianity to Scotland, met St. Mungo the patron saint of Glasgow. There is also a beautiful iron work fountain which vandals are speedily reducing to smithereens. Perhaps the spoilers would desist from their wantonness and destruction of the amenities of the city if they had a fresh look at the ancient and unabridged motto of Glasgow which simply states "Let Glasgow flourish by the preaching of the word."

The "Piskies"

Saint Andrews By The Green was built in 1750 and is the oldest Episcopalian church erected in Scotland since the Reformation. To build the church, a piece of land of approximately 1,090 sq. yards was purchased for the sum of £90 5s. This plot was situated at the juncture of the Molendinar and Camlachie burns from whence their waters mingled and flowed into the nearby River Clyde. This tiny portion of land was known as Willow's Acre and was formerly part of the Eaglesham Croft. In this rural spot which was then the outskirts of the city, the church was rapidly built in the space of one year.

The Episcopalians were mainly Jacobites and their sympathies and loyalties lay strongly in favour of Bonnie Prince Charlie. They were also unpopular with the mass of the Glaswegians who still held to the Covenanting traditions of the City. The church was built four years after the battle of Culloden and bitterness and enmity was still smouldering towards the Episcopalians or "Piskies", as they were known.

Andrew Hunter, a mason, took the contract to build the church. He was a member of Shuttle Street Secession Church which was demolished in 1845 and he was called before the church Session and questioned about his temerity in planning to build this church. He was unrepentant however and formally excommunicated.

Another martyr, on the unpopular side of the fence, was Alexander Stalker a bookseller in the City and the Editor of the Glasgow Journal. Because of his efforts in trying to raise funds for the building of the church, his sales fell rapidly and caused him financial distress.

Feelings ran high in those days against the "Piskies". especially at the rapid erection of their church in one year against the slow progress of seventeen years taken to build the neighbouring Saint Andrews Parish Church in the Square. The "Piskies" were highly suspect and one observer was reputed to have witnessed the devil actively engaged in helping to build the Episcopal

Church. "Auld Nick himself was exerting his limitless strength and heaving the heavy free-stone blocks into position as though they were feathers".

The Episcopal Church was built primarily as an English Chapel to serve the needs of the English so.diers who were stationed in the Infantry barracks near what is now Barracks Street. In the year 1805 the church was finally united with the Scottish Episcopal Church.

In the early days of the church, when the City of Glasgow was rapidly gaining in wealth and importance, it was fashionable for the Episcopal merchant princes of the city and the lairds from the surrounding area, to attend worship at this church. Indeed, to read the names on the church roll seemed like a page taken

St. Andrew's by the Green

from the Scottish edition of "Who's Who" in the landed gentry. To attend services, they smoothly rol.ed up in their carriages and on a Sunday morning, the line of carriages would stretch from the church to distant Monteith Row. Such was the zeal in those days to attend church that a family by the name of Lowndes drove all the way from Paisley to attend the services. Their enthusiasm was overshadowed however by a more lowly member of the congregation who travelled from Greenock in a coal-boat, to attend Christmas Communion.

We saw, on the panelled facing of the balconies, the names of some of the titled people who attended the church for worship such as, the Duchess of Hamilton, the Earl of Home, Lord Douglas, Sir D. K. Sandford, Garscube, Poloc etc.

The church has many interesting relics of the past. The last piece of marble from the High Altar of Iona Cathedral was saved and inserted into the Altar of St. Andrews By The Green.

There is a pair of altar candlesticks, the bases made from oak retrieved from the pilings of the old Stockwell Bridge which was constructed by Bishop Rae in the year 1345. The upper portions are made from oak recovered from the Glasgow Cast'e or Bishop's Palace which stood at the North side of Cathedral Square and now marked by a memorial stone. The candlesticks are a very rare exhibit. The four bells in the belfry were originally in the Tolbooth at Glasgow Cross.

This church also had the distinction of being the first church in Scotland to make use of an organ in the praise service since the Reformation and it was known as the "Whistling Kirk" or "Kist of Whistles". The organ was taken from its place in the rood screen of the Glasgow Cathedral in 1812 and it was purchased for £220. Unfortunately, in recent years, thieves removed the lead from the organ pipes and rendered it quite useless. It also has the further distinction of being the first church in Glasgow to be installed with gas lighting.

In 1812 the church was entered by thieves and several articles removed. The culprits were later arrested and condemned to be executed but due to the intercession of the church authorities for a lighter sentence to be imposed, the penalty was reduced to transportation.

Before the River Clyde was deepened, the church was frequently flooded and on one particular Christmas day the flood waters reached a depth of 4 or 5 feet. The St. Andrews Parish Church offered the Episcopalians the use of their church to celebrate Christmas Communion which showed a slight improvement in the relationship bewteen the two churches.

Inside the church and near the altar is a memorial to Alexander Spiers, one of the founders of the church. The plaque is unique in the fact that it states, Spiers bought the lands of Elderslie from a descendent of Sir William Wallace, the Scottish patriot.

The graveyard surrounding the church has a neglected look and appears to be the favourite place for dumping all kinds of rubbish. But, if one should care to examine the writing on the stones it would be found to be very rewarding. For instance, there is a stone to Captain Sutherland and his wife who were drowned in the steamship "Comet" in 1825. They had only been married for a few weeks. Another stone marks the resting place of Dr. Robert McNish, the author of two books which bore the intriguing titles of the Philosophy of Sleep and the Anatomy of Drunkeness. Four doctors are buried in this grave, all with the surname, McNish. The Rev. John Falconer, one of the church's first ministers served it for 57 years. He was married three times and his three wives are buried with him in the same grave. Six other ministers of the church are buried in this tiny churchyard.

Sam Bough, the famous landscape painter who was born in Carlisle in the year 1822 was a member of this church and he was married there in April 1849. Two of his pictures entitled the "Glasgow Bridge" and the "Victoria Bridge", hang in the Peoples' Palace. There is a plaque in Duke Street, opposite Burrell Lane indicating that he lived in a tenement on this site in 1850.

General Wolfe, who was stationed in the nearby barracks attended services in the church in 1753. As is known, he later lost his life at the seige of Quebec after which Canada was ceded to Great Britain in 1760.

It is to be hoped that the Glasgow planning authority will find some means by which this historic link with Glasgow's past might be saved.

Albion Street

To the casual observer the north end of Albion Street, which is situated near Marland House, Glasgow, may seem rather drab and uninteresting, its mediocrity saved perhaps from total obscurity by the periodic hustle and bustle which centres around the Daily Express dispatch offices. The hub-hub and babble of voices generally coincide with the arrival of over a million newspapers fresh from the press and ready for dispatch.

Competition is somewhat keen among the delivery men and they become rather voluble as they each try to load up their respective vans as quickly as possible and deliver the newspapers promptly for circulation in their total fleet of over 90 vehicles. In the evening gloom the ever shining bright lights, emanating from the twentieth century Daily Express building, cast a warm glow over the cobble stones in Albion Street below.

This street was opened to the public in the year 1808 but prior to this period Albion Street was church land which housed a salt market for a short time.

Contrary to first impressions gained in observing this street, it may astonish the reader to know that the street is truly a gold mine of information about this corner of old Glasgow. So much so, that recently two well known archaeologists from the Glasgow University Archaeological Department, namely Dr. Fairhurst and Mr. Talbot, decided to make Albion Street the site of their first archaeological dig in Glasgow. A lot of land measuring 6 ft. wide by 83 ft. long was marked out directly on the location of the mediaeval Greyfriars Monastery. A trench several feet deep was dug and the soil carefully sifted in an attempt to uncover any finds relating to the monastery. They were successful in laying bare a portion of the monastry wall foundations and bringing to light a variety of mediaeval pottery including green glazed earthenware from as far a field as Liniburgh in Holland, Rhineland in Germany and also France. A coffin nail, a clasp for a burial shroud and a varied collection of animal and human bones. The items found were duly handed over to the university authorities where the bones will be examined and classified by pathologists.

Circa is a latin word sometimes put before a date to indicate that the date has been difficult to determine and thus a swing of a few years in the choice of date can still be equally correct.

Circa, applied to the date of the founding of the Greyfriars Monastery, has a very wide swing indeed. It is thought however that the Grey Friars settled in Glasgow around the middle of the 13th century but a number of years passed by before they acquired the site of Barrsland in Albion Street, on which they finally founded Greyfriars Monastery, their permanent abode until the reformation.

On the 14th May, 1820, Greyfriars church was fittingly built on the grounds of the already consecrated site of Greyfriars Monastery and perpetuates the name.

The excavation revealed what were thought to be the bones of the old Greyfriars preachers who had a graveyard in this location adjoining their monastery. The bones were examined and deduced to be the bones of young men and it was also noted that the teeth were in excellent condition. They were reinterned in Craigton Old Cemetery and the site marked by a rather massive low set stone, which simply states on the stonework "Remains from Greyfriars". The human remains which the archaeologists discovered recently appear to have been overlooked in the year 1820. Greyfairs church was demolished last year owing to the redevelopment of the city.

It was in the Italian city of Assisi that the Greyfriars order was first founded by GIOVANNI BERNARDONI, better known as St. Francis of Assisi. The supreme desire of this order was to live a humble and austere life. In short they endeavoured to live a practical christian life. Other orders had fallen prey to material things of life and forgotten their high calling, best summed up in the few terse lines of verse from a poets pen :

FOR HUMANITY SWEEPS ONWARD: WHERE TODAY THE MARTYR STANDS.

ON THE MORROW CROUCHES JUDAS WITH THE SILVER IN HIS HANDS.

Many stirring incidents took place during the disruptive times of the reformation. Jeremy Russell, a Grey Friar who adopted the reformed faith, was executed near Glasgow

Cathedral in 1539. Similarly John Ogilvy a Jesuit priest was imprisoned in the Greyfriars Monastery which at this period was in use as a prison and Guard House. He was executed on the 10th March, 1615 and is buried at the north end of Glasgow Cathedral. His martyrdom is still commemorated to the present day. The Greyfriars Monastery was finally destroyed by the Earl of Argyle and the Duke of Chatelherault about the year 1560.

"Doon the watter at the Glasgow Fair", is a pithy turn of

Greyfriars Church

speech in the Glasgow dialect expressing a sail down the world-famous River Clyde. For this privilege we are indebted to the Greyfriars who instituted the Glasgow Fair which was held annually at the craigmah or craignaught, a basalt rock which lay within the bounds of the Monastery garden. It is thought the magistrates of Glasgow made many important announcements from this rock as well as decide the future date of the fair.

It is interesting to note that during the erection of the last extension to the Daily Express newspaper premises in 1957-8, the workmen had extreme difficulty in laying the foundations even with the aid of powerful electric drills which were used to penetrate the hard rugged stone believed to be the craigmah. An added hindrance was the presence of a hidden stream. However, the Greyfriars or Fransiscans did come back to Glasgow and in 1868 established St. Francis Church in Cumberland Street. The Greyfriars, in common with their early traditions, succeeded in recovering the last remaining stones from the remnant of the ruins of Greyfriars Monastery, before it was finally demolished in 1869. This was also the approximate date of the opening of St. Francis Church. The stones have been fittingly formed into a base for a cross and it is situated in the inner courtyard of the friary attached to St. Francis Church. An inscription appended states briefly thus:—

> Stones from the old Fransiscan
> Friary Founded 1476
> Near the Greyfriars Wynd
> West side of High Street.

It also further states on lettering chiselled on the stones that the Calvery or cross was erected by the Tertiaries of St. Francis, Glasgow, in the thanksgiving for the restoration of the order and a text from the Bible is finally quoted. Remember the days of old. Think upon every generation. DEUT XXXII-7.

Greyfriars Church was demolished last year as stated previously but the church hall still stands, although extremely dilapidated and apparently awaiting the demolishers to complete their task. It is interesting to observe near the corner door of the hall and in faded lettering the words "Orpheus studio". If one was permitted to climb the stairs to the top floor as indicated, we duly arrive at the one time studio of Sir Hugh Robertson, the late conductor of the Orpheus Choir. This studio was reputed to have the best acoustics of any known place in Britain. His Masters Voice company preferred to record songs here in preference to their own studio in London. Two well known songs recorded here by Sir

Hugh Robertson were:—"All in an April Evening" and "Blue-bird".

Directly across Albion Street are the premises of the Glasgow Salvage Corps, the only one in Scotland. There are only three salvage corps in Britain, one in London and the other in Liverpool. The Glasgow Salvage Corps was founded in 1873 at No. 33-37 Nicholas Street, moving to the present building in Albion Street in 1880 which they still occupy. It has been stated that sometime before 1880 the premises were tenement houses of doctors who practised in the Royal Infirmary. This may well have been true as the rooms are spacious and in many cases fitted with cunningly concealed wall safes. There are also deep basements sufficient for the high standards required for a doctor in these days.

Contrary to popular belief the Salvage Corps has no connection with the Fire Brigade. As the name implies their purpose is to salvage goods. They are financed by insurance companies and the salvaged goods are frequently auctioned off in sale rooms.

A fine example of their efficiency was the severe conflagration in 1960 at Yorkhill quay which burned down a huge shed containing 46,000 cases of whisky. The consuming flames seemed to have engulfed the shed and there was apparently little hope of saving any of the highly inflammable whisky. Nevertheless the Salvage Corps saved 17,382 cases of whisky, which adds up to a commendable 37% salvage.

By the nature of their work the Salvage Corps often work in conjunction with the fire brigade and at such a time a great tragedy befell them. This tragedy is recorded on a bronze tablet placed between Nos. 203 and 213 of the wall in front of the Salvage Corps building and it states:—IN MEMORY OF THE OFFICERS & MEN OF THE GLASGOW SALVAGE CORPS WHO LOST THEIR LIVES IN THE DISASTROUS FIRE CHEAPSIDE ST. GLASGOW 28th MARCH 1960. SUPT. E. C. MURRAY L/S/M J. A. McLELLAN S/M W. OLIVER S/M J. F. MUNGALL S/M J. C. McMILLAN. The rear windows of the Salvage Corps station windows overlook the Ramshorn Churchyard and this brings to mind an interesting encounter one of the salvage men had with a stranger who was assiduously searching for the grave of his grandfather. The stranger's name, much to the Salvage-man's surprise was that of David Niven the famous film star. If he was indeed David Niven the information is worthy to ponder over and reflect in our mind.

Revolution

In the later days of the year 1819 Glasgow was a trouble torn city. The population was seething with excitement as a radical uprising was imminent. Great hosts of unemployed workmen paraded the cobbled streets of Glasgow in regimented military fashion seeking to draw the attention of the city authorities to their sorry plight. Their demands were simple enough by modern standards: they wanted a chance to earn money to buy food and shelter.

The men had been mainly self employed at hand loom weaving and the advent of mass production at the spinning mills had thrown thousands of them out of work. The authorities of Glasgow tried hard to ease the desperate situation in these trying times. Relief centres were set up and subscriptions were invited and gathered in quickly. Consequently, work schemes were devolved to improve the Glasgow Green. Three hundred and twenty four weavers were employed at the task of levelling and sloping the fields and digging tunnels to divert, underground, the courses of the Molindinar and Camlachie Burns through large conduits on their way to join the River Clyde. However, these palliatives did not halt the cry of the people for greater reform and liberty was earnestly sought for the right to vote at parliamentary elections. King George IV and the governing classes were unwilling to grant reform to the masses considering that it would break down the constitution of the country.

In the year 1820 events came to a stormy climax. The radicals rose in revolt with the purpose of forming a provisional government. Bills, signed by order of the committee of organisation, were posted at prominent places in the city calling on the populace, at the peril of their lives, to exert their rights. The reigning government thwarted these activities by introducing trained spies among the ranks of the radicals. The spies posed as compatriots and wormed themselves into the confidence of the radicals, supplied them with arms and ammunition, deluded and betrayed them with false information and led them into a trap and, consequently to their doom.

The radical plan was to attack Glasgow from Cathkin Braes in the south and from Campsie Hills in the north and spies had circulated the information that thousands of men from England and France were ready to support them at the appointed time and place. Seventy radicals met on Fir Park which is now the Central Necropolis, and the spies directed them to Falkirk where, it was said, they would meet English supporters who would assist them to seize the Carron Iron Works, the great cannon foundry of the Kingdom. The radicals readily marched but on arrival no

Reform Bill meeting, Glasgow Cross

English supporters were to be seen and many became discouraged and left the dwindling ranks. The remaining thirty men were resting on Bonnymuir near Castlecary when suddenly a troop of the 7th Hussars advanced towards them. They refused to surrender and hastily formed a square from which they tried, with courage and poor weapons, to beat off the crushing attack of the seasoned cavalry. In the end they were nearly all wounded and taken prisoner. Carts were provided to transport the wounded to the Military prison at Stirling Castle.

Glasgow was now considered by the authorities to be the Scottish Headquarters of the Radical Movement and also became the centre of the Government instituted spy system. After the Battle of Bonnymuir the government agents speedily rounded up and apprehended the 'rebels' as they were called.

At this period of time Glasgow was heavily fortified against an invasion from the radicals. The Rifle Brigade, the 80th and 83rd Regiment of Foot, the 7th and 10th Hussars, several regiments of foot and the Glasgow Sharpshooters, a regiment of volunteers under the command of Samual Hunter, Editor of the Glasgow Herald, were called out to patrol the countryside and protect the city.

Pearlie James Wilson, a 60 year old Strathaven weaver, was the first to be arrested. He was the inventor of the pearl stitch in knitting and politically his ideas were in advance of his time. Wilson tried to make his escape unobserved through the quietness of the Strathaven graveyard at the back of his house but was discovered and promptly arrested. He was tried in Glasgow by an English court of OYER AND TERMINER and was found guilty of the capital crime of High Treason. After a trial lasting 2 days, sentence of death was duly passed in that he be "drawn upon a hurdle to the place of execution, hanged by the neck until you be dead and that afterwards your head be severed from your body and your body be divided into four quarters, to be disposed of as His Majesty shall think fit, and may God Almighty have mercy on your soul." At the appointed hour Wilson was hanged and beheaded in the Glasgow Green, witnessed by a vast crowd of 20,000 people. The greatest show of military power ever seen at an execution in Glasgow flanked the scaffold.

Amidst the scenes of this diabolical cruelty, the crowd expressed its sympathy for the doomed man by shouting in chorus "MURDER, MURDER." Perhaps the mood of the multitude foiled the executioner from quartering the body. Wilson's remains were buried in the Glasgow Cathedral Graveyard. A request by the relatives for them was refused but a hint was passed to them that the body could be easily procured. At nightfall his daughter and niece dug the coffin from its shallow grave with their bare hands and carried it back to Strathaven on an Avondale Farmer's cart, arriving at 4 o'clock in the morning. A large assembly of townsfolk was waiting for the arrival of the body of the martyr. When the body of Wilson was viewed his face was covered by a handkerchief which was let fall as a sign to the hangman that he was ready for the drop. This handkerchief is an exhibit in the Strathaven Museum. The remains of Pearlie Wilson were buried not far from the back door of his house in Castle St., Strathaven and an inscription on the handsome tombstone states: — 1846. Erected by public subscription in affectionate memory of James Wilson, a patriotic Scotsman, who suffered death at Glasgow 30th August 1820 for enunciating those principles of progress and reform by the adoption of which Great Britain has secured domestic peace and consolidated her power among the nations. Born at Strathaven 5th September 1760.

When James Wilson's house was demolished a sword, with two holes bored in it serving as a spring for his knitting equipment was found. This is thought to be the inadequate weapon he carried on his ill fated enterprise.

John Baird a weaver from the village of Condorrat and Andrew Hardie, a Glasgow weaver and ancestor of the late prominent M.P. Keir Hardie, were considered the ringleaders of the thirty men who took their stand at the Battle of Bonnymuir. At Stirling they were tried for high treason by the court of OYER AND TERMINER. The King had set up a special commission to try the radicals. The well known lawyer Francis Jeffrey took over the defence but on this occasion his eloquence was unable to save them. The fate of Baird and Hardie caused tremendous excitement among the population and influential persons sent petitions to the Government on their behalf but the King and Constitution were adamant and refused to retract the sentence of death for high treason. The executions were carried out in the same sordid fashion as Wilson's and the grizzly ceremony was enacted in the presence of the largest crowd ever to witness an execution in Stirling. Again, like the people in Glasgow, the crowd expressed its sympathy for the condemned men by shouting in unison "MURDER, MURDER." Like Wilson, Baird and Hardie faced their fate with supreme courage, declaring to the end that their cause was for truth and justice. They were buried quietly in Stirling and to make certain the bodies would not be disturbed the military guarded the grave for a period of two months. However, twenty seven years later the remains were exhumed and reinterred in the six year old cemetery of Sighthill. A massive high quadrangle tombstone marks the martyrs' last resting place, And on it is engraved:— Erected by Public subscriptions July 1847 to the Memory of John Baird aged 32 and Andrew Hardie aged 28 Who for the Cause of Freedom suffered death at Stirling 8th September 1820.

Inscribed on the remaining three sides of the tombstone is a brief history of the Radicals. The stone is sadly weather beaten, however, and the lettering difficult to read but interested parties are considering having the stone renovated. Annual commemoration services are still held a Sighthill cemetery in memory of Baird and Hardie and conducted by political groups.

Many of the Bonnymuir prisoners were sentenced to transportation to New South Wales Australia. If one cares to visit the Auld Kirk Historical Centre in Kirkintilloch, he will be privileged to examine the bundle of letters containing the pardons of the Bonnymuir victims. The letters were obtained by the well known Nineteenth Century historian Peter McKenzie from King William

IV, who instituted the Reform Bill of 1832. The letters and papers related to the period (1799-1875).

One letter in the bundle gives the following information:— John McMillan from Camelon, Falkirk, was sentenced to death for his part in the Radical rising. Afterwards the severe sentence was commuted to a free pardon on the proviso that he be transported for the remainder of his life to the coast of Australia's oldest state New South Wales. Another letter states:—John McMillan transported to New South Wales for High Treason who was granted a free pardon. Certificate of Freedom by his Excellency Leutenant General Ralph Darling, Captain General and Governor in Chief in and over the Territory of New South Wales, and its dependencies. A further interesting letter, dated 1837 Feb. 4th, written by John McMillan, 2 Windmill St., Sidney, N.S.W. to Peter McKenzie, expresses thanks to the press for having assisted him in gaining his pardon. Additional correspondence indicates that later McMillan's wife and children went out at Government expense to join him in N.S.W. A unique letter written by James Wilson is on show, protected in a glass case. It is a narrative giving, in detail, the reason why he was charged with High Treason. The letter was written in the Iron Room of the six year old Glasgow jail on 29th Aug. 1820, the day before his execution, and it is addressed to his wife. In the same show case is a copy of The Scotch Reformers Gazette dated Feb. 1837.

An interesting curio, in the nature of a life sized stone head, was discovered recently while workmen were demolishing an ancient dwelling next to the Strathaven Graveyard. In by-gone days the head with a light behind it was placed at a tiny window overlooking the burial ground. The purpose of this action was to scare off any body snatchers. It is interesting to ponder and consider that this sandstone head may be the only silent witness to the arrest of Pearlie James Wilson, who was apprehended in the nearby graveyard.

In a measure the trials of Baird, Hardie and Wilson run concurrently with the hardships of The Tolpuddle Martyrs who created a chapter in political history when six labourers from the village of Tolpuddle in Dorset, England, were transported for 7 years to Hobart in Tasmania.

Old Govan

To anyone passing through the highly industrialised district of Govan, with its miles of grey and red sandstone tenements which house the teeming population, the huge docks and shipbuilding yards which have grown up beside the famous River Clyde are readily observed. It seems extremely hard to visualise that just over a hundred years ago or more Govan was a quiet, sleepy hollow village. A slow-moving, tranquil way of life was the lot of the inhabitants, who engaged themselves in the traditional occupation of salmon fishing from the crystal clear waters of the then shallow Clyde. Latterly, the gentle art of weaving cloth for an expanding world market augmented a leisurely living.

Rip Van Winkle, the legendary figure created by author Washington Irvine, could easily have fitted into this easy-going environment and might equally have been surprised by the devastating changes which had taken place in Govan during his hundred year slumber. He would have been amazed at the transformation in the rural parish of Govan, whose far-flung boundaries now took in the Burghs of Crosshill, Govanhill, Govan, Hillhead, Kinning Park, Partick, East Pollokshields and West Pollokshields and the districts of Dowanhill, Dumbreck, Hutchiesontown, Ibrox, Kelvinside, Lauriestown, Plantation, Polmadie, Strathbungo, Tradeston and Whiteinch. Glasgow University was also within the bounds of the parish. Gorbals was under the jurisdiction of Govan Parish before acquiring status as a separate parish in 1771. But Govan Parish gradually lost much of her territory before she was finally annexed to Glasgow in 1912.

Many schools built before 1912 in the old Govan areas of Glasgow are easily recognised by a large inscription on the face of the building indicating that they belonged to Govan Parish School Board. Govan Parish was reputed to possess the richest farmlands in the West of Scotland. Many roads, such as Langlands, Broomloan, Langshot and Drumoyne are named after prosperous farms whose lands are now built upon. In addition, the beautiful mansions of Fairfield and Linthouse were situated on the banks of the Clyde, with their well kept lawns tastefully studded with trees which swept gently down to the lower waters of the Clyde. These mansions and grounds were acquired by two famous shipbuilding firms who transformed them into shipbuilding yards and gave the world the Clyde-built names of Fairfield and Linthouse.

Indeed, the entire rural area of Govan Parish, which was dotted with farms, mansions and villas, has become so heavily industrialised that now only one farm remains within its confines, namely Shiels Farm, which lies adjacent to King George V Dock,

Old Govan Village

near the river. At present, it is farmed by Mr. W. T. Fulton, whose grandfather took it over in 1875. His great-grandfather farmed Balshagray Farm and Fulton stated that what was thought to have been a covenantor's sword was discovered in the thatched roof of the old demolished Shiels Farmhouse. The present 160 acre Shiels Farm is rented from the Clyde Port Authority and it is questionable how long it will survive. Barley is Fulton's main product and it is sold to B.O.C.M. (British Oil and Cake Mills), Renfrew. In 1840 Govan Parish had 4,330 acres under crop and there were many gardens and orchards.

The village of Govan had 1,000 inhabitants in 1790, but in 1904 had grown to 91,000, thereby becoming the fifth largest burgh in Scotland. Since attaining Burgh Status in 1864, Govan's growth was phenomenal. Indeed, before being annexed to Glasgow in 1912 it was more rapid than any town in the United Kingdom or even the then new countries of America and Australia. In her heyday she was aptly called the workshop of the world and, in common with other Clyde yards, provided threequarters of the world's ships.

If we throw back the curtain of time and look back through the centuries at the story of Govan, we discover that fourteen hundred years ago St. Constantine, who was thought to be a king of Cornwall, relinquished his kingdom and devoted himself to

Christianity. He joined St. Columba, leader of the Celtic Church in Iona, and came to Clydeside to evangelise the people, first founding a church and monastery where the Govan Parish Church now stands. While endeavouring to convert the West Coast of Scotland he was martyred in Kintyre about 576 A.D. Reverently his body was brought back and buried in his own church in Govan.

In pre-Christian times sun worship was practised in this hallowed place and the Sun Stone, an instrument in this pagan form of worship, can be seen in the Stephen Chapel inside Govan Parish Church.

This church has probably the richest collection of antiquities in all Scotland. The finest example is the sarcophagus, a stone coffin with religious carvings on its sides. During digging operations for an interment in the south-east corner of the grave-yard in the year 1855 the church sexton discovered it. The roots of two large elm trees had the sarcophagus firmly enmeshed in their strong grasp. Today it is appropriately mounted in the chancel of the church with an inscription around the pedestal which simple states : " The reputed shrine of St. Constantine, King and Martyr, preserved within the ancient church, buried in the churchyard A.D. 1762, discovered A.D. 1855, placed here 1908."

There is also the shaft of the Ancient Govan Cross, with the figure of a man mounted on a horse or an ass. Scrolled on its face, a small plaque attached states that it was deposited in Govan Parish Church by Glasgow Corporation in 1928. Previous to this the ancient Govan Cross was in the possession of the Parker-Smith family of Jordanhill for almost a hundred years. Sir John Stirling Maxwell, Bart., of Pollock, was largely responsible for the church being able to acquire this interesting relic.

Also on view are five hog backed stones which appear to resemble marine creatures of the sea. They are thought to be of Scandinavian origin and may well have been headstones erected over the graves of Viking chiefs who frequently marauded the West Coast of Scotland. Incidentally, a cast of a hog backed stone is shown in The People's Palace, Glasgow Green.

Positioned at intervals along the wall of the interior of the church are ancient Celtic Crosses with their story lost in the mists of time, but which leads one to conjecture from whence they came. Situated on the wall is a memorial plaque with a list, from 1690-1929, of the Lairds of Holmfauldhead, a noted Govan family. Farther along the wall is a larger plaque indicating the names of the known clergy of the successive churches built on this hallowed site, beginning with the Celtic Church 570-1147. the Roman Catholic Church 1160-1560, and successive Protestant Church ministers since the Reformation era date of 1567. It may be interesting to note that a past minister of the church, the Rev. Roger Sandilands Kilpatrick, D.D., 1899-1912, claimed to be a direct descendant of Kilpatrick who, during the time of Robert the Bruce, was involved in the killing of the Red Comyn at the Greyfriars Church, Dumfries.

Reluctantly we leave the interior of this cathedral-like church, which was rebuilt in 1888. The previous church on the same site was erected in 1826 and its spire was a model of the church in Stratford on Avon, Shakespeare's birthplace. This latter Govan church was dismantled stone by stone and rebuilt at the corner of Logie Street and Golspie Street and is now renamed Elder Park Church.

We now find ourselves in the Kirk Graveyard, which contains over three hundred tombstones which are erected over the rude forefathers of Govan Parish. Many of the tombstones are broken and some of the epitaphs are obliterated by the action of wind and rain, but still they tell us something of the story if we but care to study the faded lettering.

Here, for instance, in the middle of the graveyard, is a sunken gravestone, tilted at an angle which states in quaint lettering :—" Here lies the corps of William Murdoch late serjeant in the Scots Fuziliers. Born in Cumlock 1717 died 1762." On the north wall of the churchyard is situated a memorial dated 1812 and the chiseled inscription solemnly declares that this burying ground is the property of John Campbell, late of the 77th Regiment. The rest of the epitaph is broken away, leaving us to surmise sadly the rest of the story. Near to the east wall is the grave of yet another soldier. The gravestone is black with age and the epitaph tells us in graphic words :—" In Memory of Lieutenant Colonel Gwyn, late inspecting Field Officer of this district, who died August 30th, 1851, aged 41, in consequence of the wounds he received in the Battles of Talavera and Busaco."

Many farmers are buried in this holy ground giving ample proof that Govan Parish was mainly an agricultural area. Numerous streets, roads and institutions in Govan perpetuate the names of farms which were in the area but now built upon.

The lettering on a grey granite tombstone, broken at the base and lying forlornly on the ground, states plainly :—" William Gardner, late farmer Greenfield, died June, 1834 aged 95 years." His farm has long since been swallowed up by the rapidly expanding Govan but Greenfield Street keeps the name alive for future generations to remember. A number of yards to the south a headstone signifies the last resting place of John Baird, Southcroft, Govan. The present Southcroft Street reminds us of this ancient steading and maintains the geographical lie of the old land of Southcroft.

A solemn tragic reminder of the primitive unspoiled waters of the Clyde and its tributaries which prevailed before the advent of heavy industries and the consequent pollution of the rivers, is forcibly brought home to us when we read the beautifully scrolled writing on two flat gravestones near the gateway to the churchyard. The inscriptions state :—" Robert Parkhill, who lost his life while bathing in the River Clyde, June, 1772, aged 16 " (presumably the Clyde at Govan), and to "Elizabeth McDonald, accidently drowned in the River Kelvin, August, 1867, aged 25." The latter

Govan from Yorkhill, 1700

leaves us to guess whether the lady was drowned while bathing or caught in a spate while fording the river. A mystery that will probably never be solved.

Residents from Hutchiesontown, Partick, Hillhead and White-inch (dates on the stones are 1824, 1762, 1862 and 1836 respectively) are buried here, giving rise to the fact that Govan Parish embraced these areas in the past.

It is interesting to note that many of the headstones include the arms of the trade Guilds of Govan. The traders were weavers, hammermen, wrights, coopers, fleshers, masons, gardeners, bonnet makers, etc. The markings are of hammers, set squares, time glasses, a press and so on. Also seen is the macabre insignia of the skull and crossbones carved on many tombstones. They appear to signify the mortality of man and the symbol of death.

To the west of the graveyard, lying against the wall, are carved memorial stones whose antiquity goes back beyond recall. They may be sections of old crosses and one can only surmise and ruminate thoughtfully their origin. Perhaps they came from some far-flung domain, brought back by a travelling missionary who treasured them highly above price.

Inside the main gateway of the Govan Parish Church stands a replica of the Govan Cross, which was built under the auspices of the Rev. George McLeod, Minister of Govan 1930-39, who did so much for the unemployed in Govan during the depression years of 1932-36.

Beneath the foundations of the Pearce Institute, which lies adjacent to Govan Parish Church, lies what is thought to be the ancient Holy well of St. Constantine. It was discovered around 1902 during the excavations for the Pearce Institute. The Holy wells played an important part in the life or the community in mediaeval times. Their waters were used for baptismal purposes and to cure the sick and consequently pilgrims were attracted to the sacred place. Not far from the well was situated the "Moat Hill," where the affairs of the district in early days were believed to have been conducted. It has long since been swept away due to building operations.

Although the salmon can no longer live in the River Clyde and has long since disappeared, the minister of Govan Parish Church still has the ancient salmon fishing rights of that portion of the river adjacent to the original Glebe.

Glasgow was made a burgh between 1175 and 1178, when many of her inhabitants made a living from the plenteous supply of salmon fished from the River Clyde. It was fitting and proper that the salmon should be displayed proudly in the Glasgow Coat of Arms.

Govan, in turn, was made a burgh in 1864. Her traditional salmon fishing industry had gone, but with foresight and energy she turned her attention to Shipbuilding and Engineering, where the ingenuity of her craftsmen turned out many of the world's finest ships.

Govan Industries

In the year 1834 a tiny Engineering Workshop was opened at 13-23 Tradeston Street, Kingston, which eventually sparked off and ignited GOVAN into the foremost shipbuilding centre in the world. The enterprise was started by two partners, Charles Randolph and Richard Cunliffe, and their first order was worth only sixpence.

In the year 1852 John Elder, to become the celebrated Shipbuilding and Engineering wizard, entered the firm and in 1854 he invented the compound engine, thereby halving the amount of coal a ship required to carry in its bunkers. This made it possible to travel greater distances and paved the way for steam navigation of the Pacific Ocean. In 1864 John Elder founded the Fairfield Shipbuilding Company at Govan on the site of Fairfield's farm and since then it has built some of the largest naval and passenger vessels that ever graced the seas.

The firm still functions under the new name of Upper Clyde Shipbuilders, Govan Division, and, true to the tradition of building fine ships, the S.G. Hopper Dredge PACIFIC was built for a Belgian firm and launched on Wednesday, 26th November, 1969. It is the largest dredger ever constructed in Britain and the shipyard workers, with exuberant enthusiasm, state that the next dredger launched will be much bigger.

ELDER PARK, facing the Upper Clyde Yard, was generously gifted to the people of Govan by Mrs. John Elder in memory of her late husband. In token of their appreciation of this action and of her husband's many outstanding qualities, the Govanites raised funds by public subscription and in 1888 erected a statue to his fine achievements and inventive skills and which had resulted in giving employment to many people in the area. The wording on the statue reads :

JOHN ELDER
ENGINEER AND SHIPBUILDER
BORN AT GLASGOW 8th MARCH, 1824
DIED 17th SEPTEMBER, 1869.

At a later date, a fine statue to his wife was erected in the Park. The Park cost £50,000 and extends to 35 acres. It was opened by Lord Roseberry on 27th June, 1885.

The Elder Library, costing £27,000 and situated at the South-East corner of the Park, was also gifted by Mrs. Elder and was opened in 1903 by Andrew Carnegie.

Mr. William Pearce became a partner in Fairfields in 1869. He was not an inventor, but had great business acumen and it was he who instigated the Atlantic Blue Riband and was successful in halving the time of Atlantic crossing by sea. He considered the Channel crossing from Dover to Calais too slow in time and he set in motion the building of the paddle ship VICTORIA in 1886, which completed the crossing in less than an hour.

At Govan Cross is a statue to Sir William Pearce. Locally, it is referred to as the Black Man, due to its black appearance. Rumour has it that it is occasionally painted and gradually, in course of time, it reverts to its black colouring. It was raised by public subscription. The readings on the four sides of the stone extol his many fine virtues, his originality of thought and marvellous skill as a man and employer of labour. He contributed largely to the development of the Navy and Mercantile marine. It was in 1887 he was created a baronet and when Govan was made a Parliamentary Division in 1885 he was elected the first M.P. He died in 1888, aged 55 years, and was buried in Gillingham, Kent.

The files of the Govan Press, dated 5th January, 1889, state that Sir William Pearce left in his will the sum of £1,200,006. His wife and son each received £500,000 and a legacy of £5,000 was left to the Glasgow Western Infirmary. It is interesting to note that in the same paper that a boy's tweed suit was advertised at 3/11 and a gent's suit a £1.

Lady Pearce, with characteristic generosity, endowed and gifted the magnificent Pearce Institute to the people of Govan.

Stephen's Shipbuilding Yard of Linthouse is also now part of the Upper Clyde Shipbuilders Consortium, but it still carries on the work of Engineering, Ship Repairing and Container Handling Equipment. Stephens Yard ceased shipbuilding in the summer of 1967 and this closed a proud chapter in the annals of shipping, as Stephens was founded at Burghead, Elgin, in 1750. It is the oldest shipyard in the world, with the exception of Scott's of Greenock. Stephen's Yard was built in the Linthouse Estate and the mansion house has been used for 45 years as offices and 5 years as canteen and welfare centre. It was demolished in 1920 and the Portico of the mansion was presented to the Elder Park, where it was rebuilt as a monument. In Stephen's administration block at Holmsfauld Road there are pictures and models on display of ships built by the Firm and also relics from the Linthouse Mansion, such as mahogany panelled doors and a fireplace which had been fitted into its new position. Stephen's have built many notable ships, but it may be of interest to mention the unique ship, SHENANDOAH. She was originally the SEA KING, built in 1863, was used as a raider by the Confederates in the American Civil War. The SHENANDOAH was instrumental in destroying 37 Federal ships and was later bought by the Sultan of Zanzibar and was wrecked off the African coast in 1879.

An appalling tragedy occurred at Stephen's Yard in 1883 when the 500 ton steamer DAPHNE, built for the Irish trade, capsized during launching. One hundred and forty-six workmen were lost.

The "Daphne" tragedy, 1883

Stephen's was ever in the forefront of progress and it is reported that the first ambulance classes, possibly in all Scotland, were started in their premises. The writer was privileged to meet 85 years old Mr. Alex. George, who can perhaps lay claim to being the oldest shipyard worker in Govan. He has served a total of 55 years in shipbuilding, including 45 years with Stephen's. He still leads a full life, particularly as an active member of the

Scottish Bowlers' Fellowship, and is also a past Deacon of the Govan Weavers' Society.

Govan has had a great share of tragedy and my attention was drawn to a small, white granite monument within the main entrance of the Elder Park. This monument is sacred to the memory of many men who lost their lives in the terrible disaster of the loss of H.M. Submarine SKELMORLIE K13, which went down in the Gareloch during diving trials in January, 1917. It was erected by the Officials, Foremen and Employees of the Fairfield Co. and gives the names of the naval Commanding Officer and Ratings, as well as those of six employees of Fairfields.

Skirting the rear of the Govan Parish Church graveyard are the empty sheds of the once famous Harland and Wolff Yards. They have lain stark and silent since 1964.

Down to the riverside to investigate the Govan claim of the one-time operation of six river ferries. It is true that services did operate across the River Clyde to Whiteinch, Partick and Finnieston; some for pedestrians and others for vehicles and pedestrian

Govan Ferry, 1800s

traffic. Only one now operates from Highland Lane and which was at one time considered a "right of way" for stepping stones existed across the river in days gone by. At the oldest and most famous, in Water Row, known as "the Govan Ferry" and thought to have been started in 1734, the closure was regarded as a breach of contract by many Govanites.

The Water Row vicinity was a favourite site for artists and such people as Sam Bough, R.S.A., W. Simpson and T. Fairbairn executed many fine works from this location. Water Row was a picturesque thoroughfare leading to the ferry with old world cottages on each side. These, of course, were demolished many years ago and tall tenements take their place.

In the main Govan Road, which leads to Renfrew, and opposite the Pearce Institute is the Cardell Hall. It is ever a source of wonder and puzzlement to the Govan people what exactly is represented by the sculptured cat holding a rat in its mouth. It is situated at a height near the guttering of the building at the junction of Govan Road and Burleigh Street. The story goes that a certain publican had an establishment with an " open midden " or refuse dumping point nearby and close to the present Cardell Hall. His cat was an exceptionally fine ratter and when his premises were finally demolished he built the present Brechin Bar with the Cardell Hall occupying the upper storey. In memory of his cat he placed the effigy in position. A few yards from this point stands an original Old Govan lamp-post, complete with the coat of arms of Govan and the insignia of the Burgh : NIHIL SINE LABORE.

Some fifty yards westward is a little square which fronts St. Mary's Church, where the Rev. James Barr at one time preached. In this square is an intricate wrought iron fountain depicting a water nymph. It was constructed by Cruishanks & Co., Denny Ironworks, and was erected to the memory of the first Police Surgeon in the Burgh of Govan.

The Clyde at Govan, 1840s

Govan Folk

Still seeking for the historical facts of Govan was becoming quite a task. The burgh was becoming younger in its inhabitants for the older people were either gone to a better place or had moved to new housing in the fringes, and their families, who might have been able to help me by hearsay had also moved away. But nothing daunted, I was able to find that the first silk factory in Scotland opened in Govan in 1824 but was removed to parts unknown when its site was taken over by an extension of the Fairfield Shipyard.

First Silk Mill in Scotland—1824

The Stage had its place in Govan. The Lyceum Theatre was opened in 1899 and Mr. Bryson, the present manager, is in possession of the first programme, printed on silk which reads: —

Tuesday, November 14th 1899.
CARL ROSA OPERA COMPANY
CARMEN   Opened by Provost Kirkwood

Most of the famous actors of the day, such as, Harry Lauder, Will Fyffe, Tommy Lorne and Jack Radcliffe performed in this theatre, but its days were numbered as a stage theatre with the advent of 'talking' pictures and it was forced to become a cinema.

At the corner of Stag Street and Govan Road is the 'Public House' owned by Kai Johanson, the Glasgow Rangers football player. He hails from Odense in Denmark, the birthplace of Hans Christian Anderson. Kai has great praise for the people of Govan, especially if initial impressions on both sides are good, and it is a joy to him that he has frequent visits from Scandinavian seamen when their ships are in port.

At 577 Govan Road are the premises of The Govan Press and as part of the architectural design of the building are the sculptured heads of Johann Guttenberg, a German printer born in 1400, Sir Walter Scott, Mr. and Mrs John Cossar, Rabbie Burns and William Caxton.

In 1875 when Govan was rapidly growing, the Govan Chronicle came into circulation. The successor of this paper was the Govan Press. Brotchie, who wrote the first comprehensive history of Govan, among many other writings, was the Editor and the Cossar family are the present owners.

There was a time when weaving was the main industry of the village of Govan and the Govan Weavers Society was instituted at Meiklegovan as Govan was then known in 1756. Their aim was to help any indigent members and their families in the area. The name Meiklegovan was used to distinguish it from Little Govan which was situated at the South side of Stockwell Bridge. It ceased to have this name about 1798 because Little Govan no longer existed as such and henceforth the name Govan was used.

The Weavers Society have various relics in their possession such as the Sherrifmuir Flag. This flag was carried at the Battle of Sherrifmuir in 1715 by a body of Govan volunteers. They were led by John Rowan of Teucherhill. Another relic is the spear of King Robert the Bruce.

The first Friday of each June is a great day in Govan for it is the celebration day of The Govan Fair. A great procession takes place, headed by a sheep's head emblem usually carried by a ship's joiner. Highly decorated lorries and carts and other vehicles form the main part of the procession, depicting the various trades of the area. Various sporting events take place on that day and one of the main events is the crowning of the Govan Queen.

There is a legend concerning the Sheep's head. A young man fell in love with a local beauty who was in service in the manse. The minister disapproved of the young man but this did not stop the elopement of the young couple. He celebrated his revenge of the minister's actions by decapitating all the sheep in the Minister's Glebe. The local people were in sympathy with the young lovers and condoned the lad's action by selecting a fine head speciman and having it duly processed and mounted to become part of the Annual Fair procession.

Coal was a great asset in old Govan. There were numerous pits in the erea such as those located where Templeton's new factory stands in the Cathcart Road; at Helen Street and Broomloan Road and with others, formed the Glasgow Coal fields They were well worked but many of them closed down in the early 19th century.

Govan had many fine mansions and not least of these was Cessnock House, in what is now known as the Ibrox district. It was situated near the place now occupied by Govan Dry Dock and was built by two brothers, Andrew and William Hunter, Glasgow manufacturers. They bought 11 acres of the estate of Heatherie Hall and built their mansion. They were related to the famous brothers William and John Hunter who respectively founded the Hunterian Museam in Glasgow and the College of Surgeons in London. They were outstanding in the medical world and were born in Long Calderwood, East Kilbride, in the early 18th century. Their East Kilbride home is now a museum.

Cessock Mansion was eventually rented to the charitable William Quarrier as a shelter for homeless boys from Glasgow and results of his work are reflected on the work still carried out at Quarrier's Homes in Bridge of Weir.

Adjacent to Cessnock was the Plantation Estate, purchased by John Robertson in 1783 who, with his brother had sugar and cotton plantations in the West Indies. Thus the Govan property was renamed Plantation from the original Craigiehall.

The district of Linthouse, until quite recently, was called the Garden of Eden due to an early tradition which forbade the granting of liquor licences and the area was, therefore, free from the existence of ale houses and such establishments. With the opening of the 'Clyde Tunnel' however, two such houses have been opened having the names "The Vital Spark" and "The Gazelle". The Linthouse Tunnel was constructed by Charles Brand & Sons during 1957-64, to act as an expressway to connect Glasgow with Abbotsinch (now Glasgow) Airport, and it cost £10M. Messrs Charles Brand states that there was nothing of archaeological interest discovered during digging operations. The South approaches were completed in 1965-67 by Melville, Dundas & Whitson at a cost of £1M plus, while the North approaches to the tunnel were completed by Balfour Beattie & Co. in 1967-69 where the costs were £1½M.

Glasgow is justly proud of its Police Pipe Band and rightly so, for it holds the World Championship record. But, strangely enough, the pipe band was founded in Govan in 1882 by public subscription and is the oldest pipe band in the world. The tartan of the kilt was a hodden grey with a box blue design running through it, but when Govan was annexed to Glasgow in 1912 an agreement was signed that the Govan Police Pipe Band and the Courts should be retained. In 1932, when Sir Percy Sillitoe came from Sheffield to be Chief Constable he attempted to make alterations in the midst of his general reorganisation, which were at difference with the agreements and had, therefore, to agree to the maintenance of the Pipe Band. Many Govan people, therefore, still regard the band as their own and as Chief Inspector Angus McDonald, the band President says, "Many Govan people still enquire how 'Their' band is progressing, particularly after it has competed in some event". The Band now wears the Royal Stewart tartan and has 16 pipers, 4 side drummers, one bass drummer and 2 tenor drums.

Another interesting fact gleaned from Constable Anderson of the Fines Department of the Govan Police is that Govan and Partick hold the unique honour of being the first towns in Great Britain to use car registration numbers by which vehicles could be identified and the owners traced. Govan commenced with U.S.I. and Partick with Y.S.I. and prior to this time, car vehicles were so few in number on the roads that their owners were known.

In the period before the advent of the steamboat and the steam engine most of the traffic passing through Govan was by road. Tolls were set up at strategic points along the way where

Paisley Road omnibus disaster, 1830

money was collected to maintain the routes and to provide an income for the owners of the roadways. A turnpike was a gate which barred the road until the toll was payed. At the juncture of Govan Road and Paisley Road West, (still known as Paisley Rd. Toll). stands an ancient iron post with a plate attached and inscribed: —

> THIS POST WAS PART OF THE OLD TOLL GATE KNOWN AS PARKHOUSE TOLL WHICH OPERATED THE TURNPIKE ROADS, GLASGOW TO GREENOCK VIA GOVAN AND TO PAISLEY VIA THE HALFWAY FROM 1780 to 1883, WHEN TOLLS WERE ABOLISHED. THIS PLATE HAS BEEN GIFTED BY THE OLD GLAS GOW CLUB. June 1934.

Not to be outdone by the existence of an Old Glasgow Club the people of Govan founded the Old Govan Club in 1914 at the Cardell Hall and T.C.F. Brotchie, Esq. was a member of the Committee.

There are few very old houses left in Govan but the Weavers Houses at 5 and 7 Stag Street are thought to be the oldest in Govan at this moment. The Stags Head Inn still functions carrying on the old traditions of the original which was situated near the Three Ells Road, so named, it is thought, because it was the breadth of three weaver's ells.

This was the hey day of the salmon fishing and the Stags Head Inn, in common with other taverns had fishing rights in the River Clyde. Salmon at this time was not considered a delicacy for it was plentiful. It was the case that servants working in local houses made it a point of employment that salmon would only be acceptabe for meals on two occasions each week. Granny Green's Cottage, in Hutchison Street, was one of the last picturesque thatched houses to be pulled down.

Highland Lane is probably the oldest right-of-way in Govan where in olden days, the highland drovers forded the Clyde at this point to proceed to the Southern Cattle Markets.

It is said that the last man to wade across the Clyde was James Knox of Seedhill Road, Paisley who carried out this daring escapade a little over 100 years ago. The story of Govan is capable of rolling on and on and possibly to an even brighter future. The outstanding achievements of the past were brought about by the application of brain and muscle and confirmed, wholeheartedly by Govan's slogan, NIHIL SINE LABORE, which simply means, Nothing Without Work, and it can be seen, when travelling through this ancient place that the will to so continue doing is there to be used.

It may well be that other parts of this great City of Glasgow have equal claim to a history such as has been briefly described here, but it is doubtful if any other district was such a great prize to Glasgow at the time of the annexation.

Granny Green's Cottage

Stag's Head Inn

The Golly or Govan Cross

Castlemilk

Castlemilk House

The Mount Vesuvius volcano destroyed the ancient city of Pompeii with fire and molten rock when it suddenly erupted in the year 79 A.D. It was tremendous news then but well-known history now.

It may greatly surprise some people to know that Castlemilk also had a volcano which many millions of years ago erupted violently and covered the surrounding countryside with molten lava and thick layers of hot ash. The sky was lit for miles around by tongues of flame which leapt from the volcano's crater as if trying to lick the low lying clouds.

Miraculously for Castlemilk, the scene has changed greatly since then. In the thirteenth century the stately and elegant home of Castlemilk was built on the site of the once angry volcano's crater which, happily for all, was now extinct. Peace and tranquility prevailed creating in themselves a place of sublime beauty. From the high battlements of Castlemilk tower could be seen a wide vista of exquisite scenery. The fragrance of flowers from the nearby gardens mingled with the scent from the avenues of the beech and fir which delightfully stirred the senses of the beholder. In the springtime the grounds near the house were carpeted with snowdrops and crocuses peeping their heads from beneath the green sod followed by the golden daffodils presenting a changing round of eye catching beauty.

Within it walls was the room in which Mary Queen of Scots slept the night before the Battle of Langside on May 13. 1568. The ceiling of the room displayed the coats of arms of Scottish Royalty and also European Royalty connected in some way with the Stuarts of Castlemilk. Mary Queen of Scots, during her short visit, took time to plant a holly tree near the house. It still flourishes profusely and a cutting from it will grow almost anywhere. Nearby on the breast of the brae is Queen Mary's.well where she is reputed to have quenched her thirst during her escape from Langside. It is interesting to note at this point that all the children born of the Castlemilk Stuart line have been christened from the waters of Queen Mary's well.

It is sad to relate that at the beginning of this year Castlemilk House was demolished. Gone are the 13th century tower and the two wings which were added in the eighteenth and nineteenth centuries. A mere fragment of the once glorious castle remains, serving as a memorial to mark the site but vandals are speedily reducing this worthwhile relic to a heap of rubble. During the demolishing of the ancient tower a secret spiral stairway was discovered in the thickness of the wall. It was probably used as a hideout in times of danger.

For twenty years before the recent destruction of Castlemilk House it was used as a Corporation Children's Home and housed about twenty children who had been neglected and abandoned and in need of care and protection. Prior to this period Castlemilk House has been in the possession of the Stuart family for well nigh 600 years. They are of lineal descent from Walter the High Steward of Scotland who richly endowed and founded Paisley Abbey in 1160.

The last of the Stuart line to reside in Castlemilk before the Glasgow Corporation bought the estate in 1935 for building purposes, was the charming Madam Helen Stuart Stevenson who carries the title Baroness of Kilbride and who is sometimes popularly referred to as Helen of Kilbride. She is the daughter of William James Stirling Crawfurd-Crawfurd Stirling Stuart, Laird of castlemilk. He died aged 82 and an oustanding chapter in the hstory of Castlemilk, which he stove so diligently to maintain, passed away with him.

Since the Corporation bought the estate they have built about 10,000 houses serving a population of 33,000 people, larger than that of Inverness. The inhabitants of Castlemilk are drawn from all over Glasgow. When Glasgow was a growing industrial city many of it's children suffering from rickets went to Castlemilk and Carmunnock which were considered health resorts, the local wells being rich in iron and lime. Castlemilk was at one time known as Castleton of Carmunnock. The original Castlemilk was situated in the Annandale beside the River Milk in Dumfriesshire and was owned by the Stuarts. They sold the property in 1579 and later resided at Casleton of Carmunnock which they re named Castlemilk.

Helen of Kilbride had two Stuart ancestors. Sir William Stuart of Castlemilk and his elder brother Sir John Stuart of Darnley who in the early 15th century went to assist the then uncrowned King Charles VII of France. In appreciation of the services they rendered, the King granted Sir John Stuart of Darnley the estates of Aubigney in the Province of Berry in France. Both brothers were unfortunately killed during the victorious Siege of Orleans in the year 1429 while under the command of Joan of Arc.

Helen of Kilbride's great grandfather, James Dennieston of Golfhill, founded the famous Ship Bank which was eventually joined with the Union Bank of Scotland and in turn united with the Bank of Scotland. The present Bank of Scotland notes have the picture of an elegant sailing vessel depicted on them in proud memory of the Old Ship Bank. The Ship Bank Inn, incorporated in the Ship Bank Building which was built in 1904 at the corner of Bridgegate and Saltmarket, Glasgow, is the site where the Ship Bank was founded. In the gardens and nursery adjoining the site of Castlemilk House is an animal cemetery. An ancestor of Helen of Kilbride, William Stirling of Keir, Captain 1st King's Dragoon Guards, fought against Napolean at Waterloo. His trusty charger lies buried beneath a yew tree in the garden. The late laird was an accomplished sportsman and his favourite dogs were buried near the yew tree. Their names, dates and apt epitaphs, composed by himself, are inscribed on small tombstones. These stones have been removed, perhaps for safekeeping.

Castlemilk district, in times past, was rich in prehistoric burial mounds which were mostly built of undressed stones. Unfortunately most of these burial mounds have been used as a convenient quarry and consequently practically all the stones were used for building dykes and farm houses, etc. Perhaps if one looks closely enough he may observe a stone of antique design built into an obscure rustic wall.

The 13th Hole at Cathkin Braes Golf Club is named Camp and it is originally thought to have been a Roman Camp. It is possible that this camp has a connection with the ancient Military Roman Road named Watling Street which is stated by Cambden's Britannia VI page 47 to have terminated at Maul's Myre in Castlemilk Estate. Cathkin Braes Golf Club was opened in 1888 and covers an area of 14 acres. Its first Honorary President was the late Laird of Castlemilk who held office from 1888-1938. His daughter, Helen of Kilbride, is the current Honorary President. A large portrait of each hangs appropriately in the lounge of the Club.

Cathkin Braes was the strategical point where a number of radicals gathered in preparation for the 1819-1820 uprising. Their plan was to attack Glasgow from the south while their compatriots, stationed on Campsie Hills, were to attack from the north and endeavour to capture the City of Glasgow. The radicals were eventually dispersed however and many of their numbers executed and transported. Cathkin Braes rises to a height of 600 feet above sea level and a spectacular view is obtained from its summit. Glasgow and its satellite towns appear to lie at your feet. Many mountains to the north can be seen

The Baroness of Kilbride, her Family and her father, the Laird of Castlemilk.

including Ben Lomond and, on a clear day, it is claimed Arthur's Seat in Edinburgh can be discerned.

As has been stated Castlemilk is rich in antiques. At the beginning of the summer of 1792, the accutrements evidently belonging to a mail clad soldier were discovered in a field near Castlemilk. The find consisted of an iron helmet, and iron neck-piece, a copper camp oven, a kettle of mixed metal, a steel dagger 28 inches long, a fragment of a leaden vase and pieces of leather belts ornamented with brass studs. The elements had eaten them away to some extent although the items were found in extremely dry land. This discovery leads one to guess whether these articles had any association within the Battle of Langside as we know the troops of Mary Queen of Scots were in this vicinity.

Helen of Kilbride made history when she was married in Carmunnock Parish Church. She was the first of the line for 600 years to be married in this quaint little village church. Her husband was Major Herbert Harry Stevenson of Braidwood, near Carluke, the seat of an old Lanarkshire family.

The Stuarts of Castlemilk sat in a special lairds loft in Carmunnock church for worship on a Sunday. Directly underneath the loft is the traditional burial vaults of the lairds of Castlemilk. It has been the family burial ground since 1470 and the Coat of Arms of the family adorns the iron grill entrance to the vaults and is ornamented with the family motto 'Avant'. Many old inhabitants of Carmunnock remember fondly the days when they were invited by the Laird of Castlemilk to his estate for their annual school trip. The horses and wagons were superbly decorated to suit the occasion and the jolly drive through the tree lined avenues culminating in a warm welcome at Castlemilk Estate. Something they won't easily forget.

Helen of Killbride fulfilled one of her ambitions when she was presented at court to King George V and Queen Mary. The pomp and pageantry was magnificent. Presentations are now no longer vogue and something of the days of gracious living has passed away.

The ancient farming area of Castlemilk was noted for the breeding of Clydesdale horses of Mr. James Clark of Windlaw Farm still carries on this tradition and that of judging horses. His father, also a Mr. James Clark, won a gold cup four times for his champion Stallion geldings in 1930. His crowning glory was in 1932 when he won the gold cup at Dundee Highland Show. He was duly presented to the Duke and Duchess of York who later were crowned King George VI and Queen Elizabeth of Great Britain. The Clydesdale horse was noted for its strength and ability to drag heavy loads and could pull easily a load of two tons through the city streets. A Clydesdale horse of large proportions might weigh between 1,800 lbs. and a ton.

Pedmyre, an ancient house situated not far from Castlemilk, is the residence of Lieutenant Colonel George Stevenson. The legend has been handed down that Mary Queen of Scots changed her horse here during her flight from Langside. Her foot became muddy when dismounting in haste and ever after the place has been called Pedmyre, a corruption from the French meaning muddy feet.

Carmunnock

MRS. BEGG'S HOUSE

Not so many years ago Carmunnock was a quiet old world village, consisting of a population of not more than several hundred people. Although it was only a few miles from the teeming metropolis of Glasgow, it still held firmly to many of its features of the past and was little affected by the social and industrial swell of its mighty doorstep neighbour.

After the Second World War conditions changed rapidly in the village and surrounding parish. House hungry Glasgow had acquired a large portion of Carmunnock Parish, including the estate of Castlemilk, for building purposes. At the same time the new town of East Kilbride took over a portion of land on the south of the Parish for industrial development. The once thriving farmlands of Carmunnock Parish, which had been tilled for centuries, were now swallowed up by the capacious maw of Glasgow and East Kilbride. Before this acquisition of almost half of the Parish of Carmunnock took place, there were approximately twenty farms within its bounds. Today only three remain, namely: PICKETLAW FARM on the BUSBY ROAD, PARKLEA FARM at KITTOCHSIDE ROAD, and WATERBANK FARM on WATERBANK ROAD. How long these farms will survive is questionable. In truth, Carmunnock is fast developing into a giant hub for through traffic serving the highly industrial and dormitory areas around. Where once the occasional horse and buggy cantered through the quaint streets, vehicular traffic has now taken precedence so much so that it has been said that 1,400 pass through during the peak hour in the morning and double this amount in the evening peak.

The name Carmunnock is thought to be derived from the Gaelic CAER MANNOCK meaning Monks Fort. The patron saint of Carmunnock is St. Cadoc, who founded the church in Carmunnock in A.D. 528. Prior to this period the druids served the religious needs of the local people. The present church was built in 1767 and is surrounded by an ancient graveyard. Situated in a sheltered nook is what is popularly known as the Minister's corner and gravestones, some of them table shaped, mark the last resting place of eleven Ministers of the Parish. The earliest date discernible on them is 1744. A stone gatehouse, built at the entrance to the church, was erected by the Rev. Patrick Glason during his ministry of 1815–24, and its purpose was to shelter the watch during the Resurrectionist period. The watchmen were duty bound to keep a sharp look-out for prowling body snatchers and inside the gatehouse, firmly fixed on the wall, is a board with a code of watch rules which run thus: 'Regulation for the watch. There are two on watch each night who are to go on an hour after sunset and continue till after daybreak in winter and till after sunrise in summer. They are strictly prohibited from getting intoxicated, or leaving the churchyard during that time and no visitor is allowed to enter on any account without giving the password for the night. They are also prohibited from making noise or firing guns except where there is cause of alarm that any of the inhabitants in such cases may be able to turn out to the assistance of the watch. Any damage that may be done to the watchhouse or furnishings is to be repaired at the expense of those who make it— ordered at Carmunnock on the 8th January, 1828.' There is a lady residing in the village who remembers that her grandfather was one of the last to take his turn at the watch.

For safekeeping the old bell of the church is lodged in the church. It was taken down from the belfry and replaced by a new bell in 1894 which was cast in Belgium or Holland and bears the maker's name MICHAEL BERGERHUYS with the date 1618. Inside the church, suitably inscribed on a plaque, are a complete list of the ministers' names of Carmunnock Parish since the Reformation in 1567. The list includes the name MATTHEW MCKAIL 1640, whose son Hugh McKail was born in Carmunnock Manse, and was a well known covenanting martyr. The name Rev. James French 1786 is also noticed. He tutored Sir Walter Scott prior to Scott's entering Edinburgh High School in 1778. In 1180 the church was placed under the authority of Paisley Abbey and according to legend, a tunnel exists between the Abbey and Carmunnock Church. The present records of the church date back to 1692.

For a small village Carmunnock has the unusual distinction of possessing two war memorials in honour of the fallen of the 1914 war. The first one consists of four beautiful stained glass church windows designed and executed by the late Mr. Norman McLeod Macdougall. The memorial figures depicted on the windows can be seen to best advantage from inside the church. The strong shapely hands and wrists of Macdougall's grandson Mr. J. D. Martin, at present residing at 65 Gallowhill Road, Carmunnock, were used as models when he carried out the work on the figure presenting the weighty sword portrayed on one of the windows. One of the names on the Roll of Honour is Macdougall's son Charles, who was killed in the Mesopotamia Turkish theatre of war, five minutes before the armistice was declared in 1918. He had served for 25 years in the 1st Battalion H.L.I. Macdougall was also responsible for planning and executing Heraldic work in the Glasgow Cathedral and the oil painting of the ascension in St. John's Episcopal Cathedral in Oban, Argyll. He is buried in Carmunnock churchyard. The second war memorial was kindly gifted by the then Laird of Castlemilk, Stirling Stuart, and is built at Waterside Road on the site of an old Toll House which served the traffic from Glasgow. This monument indicates the names of those who died in both World Wars.

Carmunnock had a second toll house which was situated at the corner of Cathkin Road and Waterside Road and which dealt with through traffic coming from East Kilbride. Many of the remaining older buildings in Carmunnock are very antique. Mrs. Begg's house for instance, at No. 8 Kirk Road, is said to date back to the 13th century, and it is generally believed that some of Mary Queen of Scots' troops lodged here shortly before the Battle of Langside. In the garden attached to this house is an ancient well, the interior of which is lined with beautifully polished brick. A window built in the chimney stack is a rare architectural feature and draws much attention. This dwelling may come under the care of the National Trust. Bishop Cottage, at 7 Rowanbank, is where the last weaver in Carmunnock resided. Directly opposite, on the site of a little green, once stood CRAIGENPUTTOCK cottage, which latterly became a tea room before being demolished. It was evidently called after the home of Thomas Carlyle, the historian, whose house Craigenputtock still stands in Dunscore parish, a few miles from Friars' Carse (Post Office Fellowship of Remembrance) in Dumfriesshire.

Adjacent to Bankhead Farmhouse, Busby Road are the famous Bee Boles, built in 1762. They can easily be seen from the main road and, as the name implies, their purpose was to protect Beehives from the wind and storm. It is said they have been much admired by bee fanciers from abroad and *The Scottish Field Magazine* has printed articles extolling their qualities.

An interesting discovery was made in the garden of the 'Craigs', Carmunnock, the residence of Mr. Greenlees, the well-known retailer. A life-sized statue of Shakespeare stands with one of the elbows resting on three volumes of books with the cryptic words ALL THE WORLD'S A STAGE inscribed thereon. The history of this skilfully sculptured figure goes back possibly to the beginning of the theatre in Glasgow. On page 54 of C. A. OAKLEY'S book entitled *The Second City* (first edition 1946) is a picture of the CALEDONIAN THEATRE, which was built in 1795 and later known as the ROYAL THEATRE, Dunlop Street, Glasgow, which shows the same statue positioned in a recess high in the top of the building. It is thought that the same statue was salvaged from an earlier building (1764–1780) between Alston Street and Hope Street on the site of the Central Station. It is said that each time the statue was re-erected as an adornment for a theatre it had the misfortune to be burned down. The statue was considered a hoodoo and ultimately it was taken to Carmunnock as a garden ornament.

Manse Road was the site of the old School House, but only the decaying walls of this one time village seat of learning remain. On the stone lintel of the doorway is the date 1736 and an earlier date 1601 is found inside the building above the fireplace. In these early days pupils had each to bring a lump of coal to keep the school fire burning.

Carmunnock has formed a splendid Preservation Society with a present membership of 300. Their aim is to preserve the delightful old village which in turn will offer a pleasing contrast to the modern but tastefully built houses which surround it. To their credit, they have purchased the old Manse Glebe and have also negotiated the purchase of the site of the NEUK adjacent to the church. The Neuk was originally a licensed Restaurant which was recently burnt down. It is proposed to make this ground a garden and consequently maintain a clear view of the village church.

Inside Boghead Public House, built in 1792, are two water colour pictures of old Carmunnock. One portrays the village and the other the 200 year old picturesque Kittoch Mill which functioned up until around 1919.

BEE BOLES

Rural Stories

Mr. Matthew Connell

Before Glasgow obtained her now world-famous water supply from Loch Katrine, Carmunnock was surveyed as a possible source but tests proved the many wells there would, in effect, only produce one third of the City's requirements.

This attempt was testimony indeed to the purity of the district's water. The Halla, Green, Matha and Doo wells formed the main supply and the latter, at Waterside Road opposite the Manse Housing estate, still provides the weary traveller with a refreshing drink. The old iron pump near-by is evidence of the bygone significance of such wells.

Possessing such a fine water supply it was natural that the inhabitants supplemented their living by hand-laundering. The advent of the industrial revolution and the introduction of machinery had quickly brought to an end the traditional hand-loom weaving. Hand laundering for the rich merchants in Glasgow thus provided a livelihood for the enterprising population. The village green was ideal for bleaching, and the Green well, now covered over, was within easy reach. It is on record that the womenfolk carried bundles of laundered clothes on their backs to Glasgow. The wages earned were roughly 8/- a week for washing, bleaching, ironing and delivery on foot to Glasgow. Mrs. McCrae, a Carmunnockonian who resides at Greenwell, Carmunnock, recollects her mother delivering the laundry to the City in this fashion. Later it was carried to Busby Railway Station and finally vehicles collected the laundry and delivered it to its destination.

As we know, the horse has largely disappeared from the rural scene and it followed that a blacksmith was no longer required at Carmunnock. Mr. Matthew Connell, now retired, is the last of four generations of blacksmiths to serve the needs of the district.

At the height of his trade an average of five horses were shod daily including repair work on harrows, ploughs, cultivators and grubbers.

On the borders of East Kilbride Parish lies Wester Kittochside Farm which is at present farmed by Mr. James Coats Reid, 10th Laird of Wester Kittochside. There have been Reids in Wester Kittochside for over 400 years and in 1773 one John Reid brought about a new system of draining land called RUMMLE which has benefited farming throughout Scotland. A book written by the Rev. Herbert Reid, M.C., M.A., for private circulation in 2 volumes, 1943 and 1945, and entitled *The Reids of Kittochside*, describes in detail the exceptional stirring history of that family.

In 1537 King James the V of Scotland granted Alexander Mure, Laird of Caldwell in Renfrewshire, the lands of Wester Kittochside. Thirty years later a successive laird, Sir Robert Muir of Caldwell, being in need of money, sold Wester Kittochside for 800 Merks to 8 purchasers. John Reid bought a sixth share of this land and paid 22/2½ Scots feu duty to his superior the laird of Caldwell. The total feu duty for Wester Kittochside was 10 merks and it was therefore known as the 10 merk land (13/4 Scots = 1 Merk). The Laird of Caldwell later endeavoured to reclaim his land. David Ure, the Lanarkshire historian, writing in 1793, aptly describes the graphic scene which took place. In 1599 the Laird of Caldwell sent out his vassals who heedlessly harried and burned down John Reid's house carrying off a considerable amount of property. One of John Reid's twelve sons was shot dead while endeavouring to extinguish the fire. After this outrage, John Reid appealed to John Lindsay of Dunrod, a near neighbour who lived in Mains Castle, East Kilbride, the ruins of which are still to be seen. This particular John Lindsay was a descendant of Sir James Lindsay, the companion of King Robert the Bruce and Kilpatrick when John Comyn was slain in Greyfriars Church, Dumfries. Mains Castle was also once the property of the Comyn family but was made forfeit on account of their adherence to the aims of Baliol and King Edward 1st of England. With influence on such a large family, he readily agreed to help John Reid. Dunrod duly presented the Scottish King with all the facts of the case which resulted in the King's desiring to see John Reid's sons. Their handsome clean cut appearances so impressed him that he announced that if any further injury be inflicted upon them, he would effect the immediate execution of Caldwell. The Reids enjoyed peace after this to till their lands, resting easily on the promise made by their King.

Thomas Dalyell, who is at present M.P. for West Lothian, is a descendant of Tam Dalyell of the Binns, also known as Bluidy Tam because of his activities against the Covenanters. The then Laird of Caldwell was a staunch Covenanter and he raised a body of horse to assist the Covenanters. When he reached Edinburgh, however, the news of the downfall of the Pentland Rising reached him. He demobilised his troops and fled to Holland, dying in Rotterdam in 1670. His lands of Wester Kittochside were confiscated and given to Tam Dalyell in 1675 in recognition of his services to King James II, but the lands were later returned to the Caldwell family at the end of the Reign of the Stuarts in 1688.

Wester Kittochside

Mr. John Perratt who, until his recent death, farmed Highflatts, built in 1713 on the Waterworks Road, stated that his predecessor recalled that Rab Ha', the Glesca Glutton, slept in his barn for the night. Rab Ha' is chiefly remembered for his exploit in successfully eating a whole calf for a wager. He died in 1843 in a hay loft in Thistle Street, Hutchiesontown, and lies buried in Gorbals cemetery.

The Bee House constructed of stone in the walled garden of Castlehill, Kittochside, and which was built in 1713, is of unusual construction. Several bee hives can be accommodated inside the bee house which serves as a protection from the elements. It has been suggested that this type of bee house originated in North Africa where they are in common use and are probably made of mud. The bees make their entry and exit through tiny slots in the walls.

Wild life still abounds in the parish of Carmunnock in spite of the advance of industry and diminishing countryside. The fox, weasel and roe deer and numerous other small animals still live in their traditional haunts. The birds are plentiful and sing just as sweetly as ever although the air is not quite as pure. Such diverse birds as the rook, owl, wild duck, kestrel hawk and swans are still seen in their natural setting, but there are only two pair of partridge left in a five mile radius. The dippers are dying out due to the pollution of the rivers and the fish are suffering the same fate. It is said that the Carmunnock area is famous for black currants, raspberries and gooseberries. Indeed the soil also produces many flowers such as the bluebells, crocuses, snowdrops, daffodils and grape hyacinths all helping to add lustre to an already beautiful countryside.

CARMUNNOCK

Carmunnock oh! how fair thy braes,
When sunrise throws its welcome rays,
O'er plantains, burns, and grassy lea,
My soul enraptured looks on thee.

Oh modern Eden, spot divine,
All your surroundings are sublime,
And every stone, and flower, and tree,
Whispers such wondrous things to me.

DORA B. NISBET

Anderston

Main Street, 1875

At 11.10 a.m. on 26th June 1970, history was made in the Anderston District of Glasgow when, with a deft snip of a royal blue ribbon, the Queen Mother opened the £11½ million Kingston Bridge, the longest in any British City and indeed the third longest in the world.

The many exuberant spectators would have been no less thrilled had they known that Her Majesty was performing this ceremony only some 80 yards from the site of the grave of a man who could also claim to possess the blood of the Royal Stewarts coursing in his veins. That man was the Rev. James Steuart, son of Bonnie Prince Charlie, whose hopes of ever wearing the crown were shattered for ever at the decisive Battle of Culloden 1746. After that historical event the name Charles naturally became unpopular in the Royal line, but after a lapse of 160 years the Queen Mother's grandson, Prince Charles, once again perpetuates it.

The Rev. James Steuart was born in Dunblane, Perthshire in 1745 and was assistant minister in St. Andrew's Church, Glasgow in 1775, being appointed the second minister of Anderston Old Church, Heddle Place which stood at the north side of Argyle Street directly under the new Kingston Bridge. He died in 1819 after a long and distinguished ministry of 44 years and was the longest serving of the nine ministers in the 200 year history of Anderston Old Church. He was buried in the church graveyard, and his obituary can be seen in the *Glasgow Courier* June 15th, 1819, page 2 column 5. It is of interest to note that Steuart's wages, according to the church records, were a stipend of £100 cash, twenty cartloads of coal valued at £2:13:4, £6 rent of the manse, bread for the sacraments, and a bun at new year 14/-. A total of £109:7:4d.

Anderston Old, built in 1770, was the first church in Anderston. It was rebuilt in 1840 and demolished in 1966 to make way for the Kingston Bridge. The remains from the church graveyard were carefully exhumed and reinterred in Section 26 of the Linn Cemetery in 1966. The remains in the adjoining North Street Cemetery were dealt with in a similar fashion and removed in 1964. It was reported that during the morbid task of exhumation in the North Street Cemetery a set of false teeth suddenly rolled out of a human skull. The teeth and plates, on inspection, were discovered to be made of solid gold and were duly reinterred in the Linn Cemetery.

In spite of the rapid disappearance of Old Anderston and the shift of the living population as well as the dead, many legends and tales still linger on about the district. Such as a bygone worthy believing explicitly that he would be reincarnated as a horse and his request to be buried standing up in the Anderston Old graveyard. This required no less than two lairs to make certain he would be able to gallop away at rebirth. His wife, not daring to share her lot with a potential horse, optioned for a different lair. Many of the tombstones in the Anderston Old Churchyard were adorned with beautiful scroll writing proclaiming to the interested passer by the names and eternal hopes, in the form of bible texts, of their silent tenants. For instance the lairds of the area and the humble weavers of old Anderston who slept side by side.

It had been stipulated by the Glasgow Corporation that the last day to apply to make claim for the remains of forebears at Anderston Old Churchyard was Oct. 25th, 1965. If unclaimed by that time, the gravestones would be broken up into rubble and used for construction work. An important stone, which covered the mortal remains of a friend of our national poet Robert Burns, was claimed from North Street Cemetery and re-erected in Linn cemetery at the new grave of the Findlater family.

The inscription on the stone runs thus—

To the Memory of
Alexander Findlater
Supervisor of Excise at Dumfries
Afterwards
Collector of Excise at Glasgow
Born 1754 – Died 1839
The Friend of Robert Burns in Life
His Vindicator After Death
Erected By
Sandyford Burns Club. 1923
Other Members of
The Findlater Family
Also Are Interred Here.

Anderston Old Church in Heddle Place possessed many fine furnishings and worthwhile antiques dealing with the past life of the city. Many of these items were saved before the church was demolished and were distributed to other churches in various parts of the country. The pulpit was beautifully carved with Jacobite Roses, perhaps in honour of the Jacobite lineage of the Rev. James Steuart, who ministered during this period. This pulpit was gifted to the Free Church in Stornoway.

The church had the honour of being visited by Mary Slessor during 1848–1915. She was the Aberdeen girl who served in the mission field of Calabar, Nigeria. The seat she occupied is still greatly prized and was ultimately shipped to the Free Church in Dumbarton. Eliza Jane Aikman, a daughter of the Rev. John Logan Aikman, D.D., fourth minister of Anderston Old, was the founder of the Infant Health Visitors' Association, which has developed and grown into the present Corporation Child Welfare Department. A plaque to her memory could be seen in the vestibule of the church before its demolition. It has now been removed to the People's Palace Museum, Glasgow Green.

The remains from the graveyard at St. Mark's Church, Cheapside Street (opened in 1793 and originally the Seccession Church) were in 1964 reinterred in Section 22 Linn Cemetery, thus completing the vast task of removing the dead from Anderston. It was the first major undertaking of this nature carried out in Glasgow since the start of recent large scale redevelopment within the city. Henry Bell (1767–1830), who built the first steamship the 'Comet' and who was a pioneer of steam navigation, married Margaret Young in the church. It was the first marriage to be celebrated there. In 1827 this church was transferred to Wellington Street where the Alhambra Theatre now stands. Finally the church was removed to University Avenue where it is now known as Wellington church.

The Kingston Bridge forms a complex of sweeping bridges and roadways which are predicted to carry 70,000 vehicles per day by 1970 and 120,000 per day by 1990. Wandering around the forest of giant columns supporting the mighty bridges, one could perhaps be justified in imagining himself a Lilliputian completely dwarfed by the all powerful transport network and that Anderston was indeed fast becoming the traffic hub of Glasgow. It may surprise some readers to know that it was prophesied by Andrew Peden (1626–1686), the noted Scottish Covenanter and sometimes referred to as 'Peden the Prophet', that the 'Cross of Glasgow' would, in the future, be at Cranstonhill Anderston. His prophecy is well on the way to being realised.

Peden's Cross was at one time engraved on the corner of the former handsome building at the juncture of Elderslie Street and Argyle Street. It was thought to have been built by a past Baillie of Anderston in 1856. The voyages of time and weather have worn the lettering away. A stone bust, situated high up in the corner of the building, is reputed to be that of Peden with his sightless eyes appearing to look towards the Kingston Bridge and contemplating his prophecy come true.

The old Anderston Weavers Society Building, erected in 1865 and which stood on Argyle Street, was swept away on 8th September 1967, to make

Peden's Corner

way for the new bridge. Newspapers and coins, which were found in a large glass bottle sealed in the Keystone retrieved from the foundations of the building, included an 1840 Queen Victoria groat or 4d piece and an 1845 crown or five shilling piece. They are now on show in the ground floor east room of the People's Palace Museum. For a hundred years Anderston was famous as a weaving village and the weavers, in order to protect their interests, established the weavers' Society of Anderston on 3rd November 1738. The Weavers' Society intend incorporating the memorial stone, which was taken from the demolished Weavers' Building, and the Society's Coat of Arms in a new building, the site of which has not yet been decided.

Cranstonhill, referred to by Peden as the future Cross of Glasgow, was in earlier times known as Drumover Hill, originating from the Gaelic meaning Grey Ridge Hill. An earlier legend states that Drumover Hill was the appointed place where the vagabonds from Glasgow were dispersed after being expelled from Glasgow city bounds. They were marched out of the city to the rhythmic drum beat of the 'Rogues' March'. Hence the early Glaswegians' name of Drumover Hill. Cranston Hill estate was owned by Henry Houldsworth, the first Provost of the Burgh of Anderston in 1824, and Houldsworth Street was named after him. St. John's Church, standing at the corner of Houldsworth Street and Argyle Street, was founded by him in 1849. Alexander J. D'orsey, first Principal Teacher of English at the Glasgow High School, appears to have been a founder with Houldsworth. D'orsey was installed as the first minister of the church which is scheduled for demolition. A few of the church furnishings are now in use at St. Andrew's by the Green Episcopal Church, Glasgow.

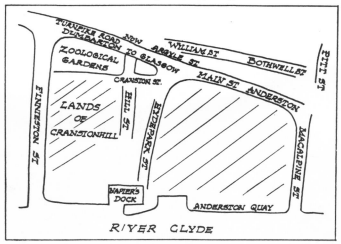

Anderston 1839–40
(reproduced from a map by A. MacFarlane)

Early Days

Blaeu's Atlas, 1654

Tranquillity reigned supreme in the huge forest. The trees echoed the sweet songs of birds and high overhead could be seen the Golden Eagle and the White Tailed Eagle circling in the air, with the GOSHAWK searching for prey and the OSPREY catching fish from the River Clyde. The beavers were busily engaged in building dams in the Blythswood Burn and the red deer and the roe deer were bounding through the forest.

Suddenly the peace was shattered by the howl of a pack of wolves. As all bedlam broke loose, the discordant flapping of wings, and the excited squawking of birds mingled with the crashing of wild animals through the undergrowth intent on getting to safety out of the way of the killer wolves. A wildcat, crouched on the overhanging bough of an ancient oak, was hissing, spitting and lashing the lair with its bushy tail ready for instant action at the impending danger. Keeping safely in concealment it watched warily and suddenly before its gaze a family of squealing and grunting wild boar broke from the secluded shelter of a clump of scotch fir trees, raced furiously underneath the bough of the watchful wildcat, only to disappear into a thicket of alder trees. A few moments later the pack of ravenous wolves, their howls now rising to a frightening crescendo, followed like black wraiths in hot pursuit of the wild boar.

Scenes such as these were common occurrences among the denizens of the Bishop's Forest which partly circled Glasgow, stretching from Parkhead to Hamiltonhill with the River Clyde its southern boundary and, of course, present day Anderston lying within its confines. The Bishop's Forest, where the Bishops of Glasgow used to hunt, disappeared many centuries ago and that part of the forest which is now Anderston is a forest of concrete columns supporting the Kingston Bridge, tall multi-storied buildings, and a varied collection of factories. The area is now devoid of parks and has few trees.

A charter states that the Bishop's Forest was granted—by King James II in 1450 at Edinburgh the 20th day of the month of April in the year of our lord and 14th year of our reign—to William Turnbull, Lord of Provan, Bishop of Glasgow and founder of the Glasgow University. It may be of interest to readers to know that the last wolf killed in Scotland was by a Brora, Sutherlandshire huntsman in 1700. A stone was erected to commemorate this incident in 1924.

Anderston's new forest of columns

In the year 1721 the aspect of the rural district of Anderston changed rapidly. The Andersons of Stobcross were a prominent and ancient family owning Stobcross as far back as the reign of James VI. James Anderson decided to build a village on an unproductive section of his land in the years between 1721–1735. When the hamlet was completed it was named ANDERSONTOWN after its builder, later becoming better known as ANDERSTON. In 1735, a successive owner of Anderston, John Orr of Barrowfield, Bridgeton, extended and improved the village. (Orr Street in Bridgeton is named after the Orr family.) In 1721 the first house in Anderston was built at the juncture of North Street and Argyle Street by John Stobo and was referred to locally as the Old House. Stobo was one of the first manufacturers in the field of commerce and one of the founders of the Anderston Relief Church. Strangely enough he was the first to be interred in the Anderston Relief graveyard and, as has been stated previously, the remains are now reinterred in Linn Cemetery. Stobo's old two-storied house was demolished in 1892.

It might be imagined that the name Stobo gave rise to the name Stobcross but such is not the case. Stobcross took its name from an ancient wooden cross which stood at the junction of Finnieston Street and the main highway which ran between Bishops' Palace, Glasgow and Partick.

The population of the village of Anderston in 1791 was around 4,000, and although it was rapidly becoming an important industrial centre, it was still mainly a rural area. Within and bordering the parish were many country estates namely Hydepark, Overnewton, Kelvingrove, Napiershall, Lancefield, Thornbank, and farms such as Pointhouse, Sauchyhall and Sandyford. The Mansion House of WHITEHALL was the residence of Hugh Niven, ancestor of David Niven the famous film star. It is obvious that many of the main streets and districts of Anderston were called after these former country estates and farms which are, in most cases, now built upon by factories and houses. In 1795, when Glasgow was a small town, there were 146 Gentlemen's estates within a seven mile radius of Glasgow's borders. Since then they have been mostly swallowed up by the City.

The village of Finnieston was built by Mathew Orr in 1768 and became a holiday resort for the wealthier citizens of Glasgow who delighted in the quiet solitude and the leisurely pastime of salmon fishing from the then crystal clear waters of the Clyde. Finnieston, known as World's End, possibly because of its remoteness, was called after the Rev. James Finnie, who was a sometime tutor of the Orr family. Among the earliest to own a house in the village of Finnieston was John SMITH, who started in business with a circulating library, and since then the firm has become one of the best known and oldest book establishments in Scotland.

Anderston owed its spectacular industrial development to a few men of foresight and drive who were quick to take advantage of the industrial revolution. The practical introduction of steam power by James Watt, who was born at Greenock in 1736, made it easy to harness water power for industry, and consequently the building of factories in turn superseded the work previously done in the home. William Gillespie, who pioneered the first calico printing works in Anderston in 1772, built a mill, in Mid-Woodside on the River

Kelvin, which employed many people in Anderston. James Monteith, who was born in 1734 at Bishop Street where his father operated a market garden, erected a spinning mill in Bishop Street in 1750. It lay off the main road and was the first side street to be built upon in Anderston. In 1780 Monteith was the first in Scotland to weave pure cotton, and his portrait painting is in the custody of the Old Anderston Church authorities.

Henry Houldsworth from Nottingham was appointed by William Gillespie and Son to take charge of their mill at Woodside and, taking advantage of the great increase in trade, Houldsworth decided to start in business for himself, building a mill at Cheapside Street. His success brought him much fame and fortune. In 1777 GLASGOW PROVOST PATRICK COLQUHOUN (1782–84), in partnership with COOKSONS of Newcastle, opened at Finnieston the VERREVILLE crystal factory, the first of its kind in Scotland. The work done here was very high grade, and fine examples of verreville china can be seen on the MID floor of the People's Palace Museum, Glasgow.

Soon people flocked to Anderston from the surrounding country districts to obtain work. Immigrants came from Ireland to escape the terrible potato famine in 1846–47, and many people from the Highland clearances found their way to Anderston which consequently rose rapidly from a quiet village to a booming town. It was a proud day for Anderston when on 24th June 1824 it acquired Burgh status by the granting of a charter by George IV. The population was around 10,000 at this time, but Anderston only enjoyed this privilege for a period of 22 years, probably the shortest Burgh status on record in Scotland, before being annexed in 1846 by the ever encroaching City of Glasgow.

Anderston burgh had nine Provosts, and it is on record that a SCROLL giving an account of the then Anderston Town Council was rescued from the foundation stone of the Anderston Old Church demolished in 1966. The scroll refers to John Miller, 6th Provost of Anderston (1839–40), as Lord Provost. Sir James Lipton, born in Glasgow in 1850, founded what was to become, at that time, one of the largest retail businesses in Britain. His second shop was in effect opened in Anderston. Sir Thomas was a keen yachting enthusiast and competed for the America Cup. Many of his trophies can be seen in the People's Palace Museum.

Although Central Anderston has been swept away in the march of progress, many buildings of considerable merit still remain perhaps in time to suffer the same *coup de grace*. The Cranston Street Police Court building, erected in 1870, has two fine life sized statues adorning its façade. They are possibly indicative of truth and justice. The old Marine Police Station at 25 McAlpine Street has the Coat of Arms of Glasgow above its doorway but is now the premises of the D. S. BADDELEY ENGINEERING Co. Ltd. The original thirteen prison cells can still be seen inside the premises, grim reminders of the past. The Shandon Bells and Buttery at 654 Argyle Street has on show inside snow skis that are reputed to be the oldest in Scotland. They were a gift of Dr. Hepburn, ex owner of the Red Hackle Scotch Whisky firm. The Shandon Bells occupy the lower part of a building, built in 1869, which appears to have been erected by the Free Masons because sculptured on the face of the building, which is to be preserved, are Free Mason symbols.

Cranston Street Police Court Building

Going west from Glasgow along Anderston Walk (now Argyle Street) one would have passed the village of Grahamstown which possessed only one street, running north and south, known as Alston Street. This is where the first permanent theatre in Glasgow was built in 1764. Grahamstown is now covered by the Central Station, but it is thought by many people that Alston Street still exists beneath the foundations of the station. It is also reputed that quantities of silverware were left abandoned in the shops of this street and never claimed. The Salvation Army building at 724 Argyle Street, erected 28th May 1904 and designed by Mr. J. Hamilton, is probably the only building in Anderston which can boast ten foundation stones. They can readily be seen on each side of the main doorway and were laid by a notable person. Lieutenant Colonel Bonnyface of the International Salvation Army Headquarters, London, states that these stones were laid by people of goodwill who had subscribed towards the funds of the Army.

Modern Anderston

The Anderston Savings Bank at 752-6 Argyle Street, built 1899–1900, was designed by James Salmon II. It is a splendid red sandstone building. The doorway, with a semidome of blue mosaic, is reminiscent of a church sanctuary, and is considered one of the finest doorways in the United Kingdom. The banking hall has a specially fine fireplace depicting the figures of St. Andrew and St. Mungo and was sculptured by Albert Hodge. The building, although previously scheduled for demolition, will now be saved.

The Queen's Dock, which has served Glasgow for so many years, will soon be filled in, but Glasgow Corporation have not yet decided what will be done with this valuable site. The last coping stone laid in the construction of this dock is situated at the brink of the dock at the Finnieston Street end and on it is inscribed—

THIS DOCK
BY KIND PERMISSION OF HER MOST GRACIOUS MAJESTY
QUEEN VICTORIA.
NAMED
QUEEN'S DOCK
THIS THE LAST COPE STONE LAID ON THE 20TH MARCH A.D. 1880
BY THE HON. LORD PROVOST WILLIAM COLLINS. CHAIRMAN
DAVID ROWAN DEPUTY CHAIRMAN OF THE COMMITTEE OF
MANAGEMENT

Nearby on the Finnieston Dock stands a huge crane. A notable landmark, it is reputed to be the largest in Scotland. Not far away is the Anderston entrance to the Harbour pedestrian tunnel built in 1895. This tunnel runs under the Clyde from Anderston to Govan, and there are 138 steps down to the floor of the tunnel at the Anderston end and about the same number at the Govan end. At one time there were two vehicular tunnels running adjacent to the pedestrian tunnel but they were closed during the 1939–46 war. The tunnel entrance is falling into a rather sad state of decay and is a favourite haunt of starlings and pigeons. It is to be hoped it will not be closed as it is still useful to pedestrians and is an unusual reminder of the past.

Inscribed on a stone at the gable end of Fitzroy Place, Claremont Street, adjacent to Trinity Congregation Church, are the words—

GLASGOW BOTANICAL GARDENS

INSTITUTED 1817

THE GARDENS REMOVED

TO THEIR PRESENT SITE

1842

As previously stated, this was the site of the original Botanical Gardens. The last tree from the original gardens was transplanted in Kelvingrove Park where it is thought to still exist standing on a mound near Kelvingrove Gate. There is also a Weeping Ash tree near the main lawn in the centre of the present Botanical Gardens which was transplanted from the original site. This tree has a tag attached giving such information.

Many of the old well-known and established firms of Anderston were forced to move to other parts of the district due to the upheaval caused by the redevelopment of the area. Among them was James Buchanan & Co. Ltd., Washington Street, proprietors of Black & White Scotch Whisky. The firm moved to a new site in Stepps. The Washington Flour Mills of G. R. Snodgrass, 10 Anderston Quay, is one of the foremost flour mills in Scotland. It has seen management by five generations of Snodgrasses. The founder was a farmer who came from Knock Farm, Renfrew.

One day in 1821 an American ship 'Morning Star' sailed up the Clyde and docked at the Broomielaw. This was just nine years after Henry Bell's 'Comet', the first steamer to make the then spectacular journey from Greenock to Broomielaw in 3½ hours. The Captain of the 'Morning Star' proceeded to invite seamen to religious services aboard his ship. These services inspired many people to help the seamen as their lot was very hard in those days. Consequently a movement was started and the Seamen's Friend Society was founded in 1822. Two years later the headquarters and adjoining Church of the Society were duly built.

It has been brought to light, after a three years' world-wide research conducted by a Norwegian Minister, Rev. Roald Kvernal, that the Seamen's Friend Society is the oldest in the world. During the disastrous fire in James Watt Street on Monday 18th November 1968, when 22 people lost their lives, Mr. J. A. Stewart, J.P. Superintendent of Seamen's Bethel and his staff, provided food and shelter for the relatives while they waited to identify kin lost in the fire. They also provided for the policemen and firemen on duty. The Bethel received a vote of thanks in Parliament from the Secretary of State for Scotland and were also thanked publicly by the Lord Provost of Glasgow.

What will be one of the biggest and most modern Newspaper Plants in Europe is at present under construction for the *Daily Record and Sunday Mail* at Anderston Quay and will be completed in July 1971. During excavations for the foundations, what was thought to be the crypt of an old church was discovered in the sandy soil.

The Clyde Port Authority at 16 Robertson Street is a finely sculptured building, the architect being Sir John A. Burnett, A.R.S.A. Inside the building hangs a notable picture by Sam Bough, the painter, and on a brass tag attached is stated—

SUNSET ON THE CLYDE

BY

SAM BOUGH 1862

PRESENTED BY SIR THOMAS DUNLOP B.T. G.B.E. 1933

Shipbuilding on the Clyde at Anderston has long since ceased, but it may be of interest to mention the former yards. David Napier, the shipbuilding wizard, moved his shipbuilding business in 1822 from Camlachie to Lancefield Quay, Anderston. Napier's managers, David Tod and John McGregor, left his services and formed a partnership, and founded Tod & McGregor Shipbuilding yard, Meadowside, west of Broomielaw. In 1872 Messrs. Handyside and Henderson purchased Meadowside Shipyard and Engine Works at Warroch Street, the firm later becoming known as D. & W. Henderson. They built fine ships including yachts, and there the super yacht 'Thistle' was built specifically to challenge the America Cup. Latterly it was sold to the German Emperor Wilhelm II and renamed 'Meteor'. During 1936 D. & W. Henderson's Shipyard, Meadowside, was taken over by Harland Wolff. A. & J. Inglis, Shipbuilders, owned the Pointhouse shipyard which had originally been founded by Thomas B. Seath in 1847. T. B. Seath transferred to Rutherglen to carry on shipbuilding there. Anthony & John Inglis had previously been engaged as Marine Engineers with Tod & McGregor, Meadowside. Inglis built a variety of ships including the famous Clyde paddle steamers 'Kenilworth', 'Marmion', 'Talisman' and 'Waverley', all named after Sir Walter Scott's novels. This firm was also taken over by Harland and Wolff. Robert Barclay also had a shipyard at the foot of Finnieston Street at what was then known as Pointhouse Road.

The Western Fire Station in Cranston Street will soon be demolished and rebuilt in Kelvinhaugh Street. The crew of this fire station were the first to be notified and turn out to the two major fire disasters: the whisky bonding warehouse fire on the 28th March 1960, where a total of 19 firemen and salvagemen lost their lives, and also the previously mentioned James Watt Street fire. The station is said to be the oldest in Glasgow.

At the corner of Carrick Street and Crimea Street was situated the house, recently demolished, where William Simpson, the famous painter, was born in 1823. He painted many scenes of Glasgow which can be seen in the People's Palace. Simpson joined the staff of Messrs. Day & Son, London, in 1855, and his duty called him to make sketches of the Crimea consequently earning him the name of 'Crimea Simpson'. He was acquainted with Florence Nightingale.

Even the lodging houses in Anderston have their graphic stories to tell. Jim Higgins, Bantam Weight Champion from Burnbank, Lanarkshire, and holder of the coveted Lonsdale belt won three times in the unusually short period of 11 months, gained riches and fame as a boxing champion, but was sadly latterly reduced to living in the lodging houses of Hydepark Street and the Popular Hotel, Holm Street. Jim was found dead in a narrow pen off 327 Argyle Street, friendless and penniless.

Jackie Paterson, the former Fly Weight Champion of the world, who was reported to have earned the sum of £90,000 at his profession and who died in South Africa in 1966 aged 47, fought in the Kelvin Hall and trained in Kelvingrove Park.

Cheapside Street, Hydepark Street opened 1790, Piccadilly Street, Whitehall Street and also Charing Cross, are named after streets in London. Sauchiehaugh Street was at one time lined with Sauchs (Scots word for willows). Sauchie means abounding in willows, but the word has obviously been corrupted into Sauchiehall Street. Stobcross Street was originally the tree lined avenue leading into Stobcross House, and surprisingly enough Stobcross Street is again being made into an avenue of trees. Grace Street was named after the youngest daughter of John Geddes of Lancefield House and Manager of the Verreville Pottery. She was accidently fatally burned while getting ready for a dance.

At one time the boundaries of towns in Scotland were marked by what were known as boundary, Royalty or March stones. Anderston was no exception and it had 210 march stones marking off its borders. Stones 208 and 209 existed until recently at 492 and 453 Argyle Street. Fortunately one has been saved and along with about 40 other antique stones is at present in safe custody at the Corporation Building Yard at Ellesmere Street, Glasgow.

The first tramway route in Glasgow was from St. George's Cross to Eglinton Toll and was opened on the 19th July 1872. Control of the tramways was taken over by the Corporation on 1st July 1894. Anderston formed part of the sixth route which traversed between Whiteinch and Bridgeton Cross, and it was necessary to employ trace horses to haul the tramcars up the steep brae at Coustonhill. The last tram car in Glasgow was taken off the old No. 9 route (Dalmuir West to Auchenshuggle) on 4th September 1962.

Napoleon I, Emperor of the French, was indirectly responsible for raising the Anderston Volunteer Corps when he threatened to invade these shores. The Corps formed one of the eight regiments of the Glasgow Light Horse raised in 1803, and consisted of eight companies, 32 officers and 500 rank and file. They were known locally as the 'sweeps' and proved efficient troops. John Geddes of the Verreville pottery was Colonel commander, and the Rev. James Stewart, who was responsible for publishing a book entitled *The Banners of Britain to assemble her Brave Warriors*, was chaplain.

The Provost's chain of the old burgh of Anderston, which originally belonged to the weavers' society of Anderston who gave permission to the Provosts of Anderston to use it for ceremonial occasions, has been missing for 121 years. In the People's Palace at present are on display the Provosts' chains of Partick, Govan, Pollokshields (ceded to Glasgow 1912) and Kinning Park (ceded in 1905). The Burgh of Anderston appropriately adopted the basic coat of arms of the Andersons of Stobcross, after whom the town was named, with a few additions. For instance, a leopard with a spool in its mouth flanked with a craftsman and a merchant indicating trade and commerce and the crest of a ship in full sail representing foreign trade. Since then Anderston has lived truly up to her motto

'The one flourishes by
the help of the other'.

Gorbals

Glasgow from Gorbals, 1700s

There are few places in the world which have been as much maligned as the district of Gorbals in Glasgow. References have been continually made to the appalling slums, overcrowding conditions and all the attendant evils which prevail within the borders of Gorbals.

Press and literary men have never tired of setting down in print their grim impression of this so called blighted area, and the book entitled *No Mean City*, written by A. McArthur, a son of this area, has gained a very wide circulation. It readily turned the spotlight of publicity on the sordid side of Gorbals and helped shoot the flames of prejudice sky high. But conditions in Gorbals were not always so. Around 1800 this was where the rich merchants of Glasgow desired to buy the splendid Georgian type houses. Gorbals was then akin to Newton Mearns on the outskirts of modern Glasgow and, as has already been written, Gorbals was originally part of the Parish of Govan, being made a separate parish in 1771. The Gorbals parish was of small extent then comprising 28½ acres, but in 1886-7, according to John Bartholomew's Post Office Directory map, it had grown to 42 acres, 1 rood, 17·3 poles. The present area of Gorbals now covers 272 acres and can be compared to a good sized dairy farm.

The first family of note featuring largely in the early days of Gorbals were the Elphinstones. William Elphinstone was the founder of Glasgow's foreign trade, and during the reign of King James I (1424–1437) set up as a merchant in Glasgow and exported cured salmon and herring to France in exchange for salt and brandy. Another member of this wealthy family was John Elphinstone who became a Baillie of the city of Glasgow in 1512. He is thought to be the same John Elphinstone who was tenant of the lands of Gorbals. Later the tenancy passed to a descendant, George Elphinstone who, in 1579, converted the rent into feu duty. His son, also named George, knighted in 1594 by King James the VI, was elected provost of Glasgow in 1600 and eventually represented Glasgow in the Scottish Parliament. His lands at this stage were, by a charter granted by Archbishop Boyd, made into a free barony under the Crown.

Gorbals Cross

George Elphinstone, Senior, built the turreted building known as the Elphinstone Mansion which was, for long, an enduring feature of the old Gorbals. It was situated at the corner of Gorbals Street and Rutherglen Road. An adjacent building was built in 1634–35 by Robert Douglas, Viscount Belhaven, who bought the land at this period. His coat of arms was fashioned deeply in the stonework. In 1636 Viscount Belhaven settled the lands of Gorbals on Sir Robert Douglas of Blakerston, who was married to Belhaven's daughter, but in 1650 the town council of Glasgow purchased the lands of Gorbals for £6,777-15-6 from Sir Robert.

The dreaded disease leprosy was prevalent in Scotland in the middle ages, and in 1350 the devout Lady Lochow, her maiden name Marjorie Stewart, built on St. Ninian's Croft a leper hospital and dedicated it to St. Ninian. It was situated near the bridge in Gorbals Street and a graveyard which bordered Adelphi Street was attached. A few years ago, when workmen were laying foundations for a garage on the site of the graveyard, remains were discovered which were thought to be those of lepers. Each leper was supplied with a bell and when out walking rang it chanting 'Unclean, unclean' to warn people not to come too close. It would be imagined that, in these days, living in Gorbals was not very popular. However, the leper hospital was demolished in 1730. A chapel was built near the Elphinstone Mansion in 1494 by William Steward, a canon of Glasgow, and the lepers residing in the hospital had to ring the chapel bell every night and pray for their guardians. The chapel along with the Elphinstone Mansion was demolished in 1867.

There are now three main River Clyde bridges which link Gorbals with the north of Glasgow, but in very early days there was no bridge and the river, which was then very shallow, could be forded at certain places. The first stone bridge across the Clyde was from Stockwell to the village of Gorbals and was built by Bishop Rae in 1345. Previous to this it was reputed that in 1285 a wooden bridge existed but it fell into decay in 1340. The present bridge known as Victoria bridge was opened in 1854. Bishop Rae's bridge served Glasgow for well-nigh 500 years, and this old bridge must have witnessed many of the stirring scenes of old Glasgow. The Regent Moray crossed this bridge with 600 Glasgow men among his troops to defeat his half-sister Mary Queen of Scots at the decisive Battle of Langside in 1568. Prince Charlie would have used the bridge when he was in Glasgow for ten days with his troops in 1746 before proceeding north to Culloden. He was known to have visited Gorbals on this occasion. It would have also given a passage to Archbishop Beaton when he escaped to France with the Glasgow Cathedral's records and precious church relics during the Reformation. Robert Burns, our national poet, must have treaded its ancient arches on his way to visit the city and for his stay at the Black Bull Hotel, Argyle Street. The Highland Host, during covenanting times, passed over the bridge in their bare feet, and the metal girt wheels of the London-bound stage coach would ring on the old stone bridge as it raced furiously to its distant destination. The bridge was the central point for vendors and beggars who battened on the travelling public. A few relics of the Bishop Rae's bridge are still in existence. The wooden altar candlesticks, at present in St. Andrew's by the Green Episcopal Church, are partly made from the old oak piling, and a large table situated outside the City Librarian's Office on the Mezzanine floor of the Mitchell Library also came from the piling.

The Victoria Bridge superseded the Bishop Rae's bridge which was demolished in 1847. It is called Victoria Bridge in honour of Queen Victoria, cost £40,000, and is supported by five arches. Jamaica Street Bridge, sometimes known as Broomielaw Bridge or Glasgow Bridge, has its story inscribed on the inner central parapet. Above the inscription is the coloured Coat of Arms of Glasgow and the inscription reads as follows: THE FOUNDATION STONE OF THE FIRST BRIDGE WHICH WAS 30 FEET WIDE WAS LAID ON 29TH SEPTEMBER 1768 BY PROVOST GEORGE MURDOCH. OPENED FOR TRAFFIC ON 2ND JANUARY 1772. ON 3RD SEPTEMBER 1833 THE FOUNDATION STONE OF THE 2ND BRIDGE WHICH WAS 60 FEET WIDE WAS LAID BY JAMES EWING, ESQ. MP FOR THE CITY. OPENED FOR TRAFFIC 1ST JANUARY 1836. THE FOUNDATION STONE OF THIS BRIDGE WHICH IS 80 FEET WIDE WAS LAID ON 8TH OCTOBER 1896 BY LORD PROVOST SIR JAMES BELL, BART. OPENED FOR TRAFFIC ON 24TH MAY 1899 ON THE EIGHTIETH BIRTHDAY AND THE SIXTY SECOND YEAR OF THE REIGN OF HER MOST GRACIOUS MAJESTY QUEEN VICTORIA. SIR DAVID RICHMOND LORD PROVOST JOHN MCFARLANE ESQ. JP CONVENER OF THE BRIDGES COMMITTEE.

The first bridge across the Clyde joining Saltmarket with Crown Street was called Hutchestown Bridge and was opened in 1792. It was just newly completed and barely in service when in 1803 it was demolished by a flood. A light wooden bridge was then built and in 1829 was replaced by a third bridge which was dismantled in 1858. It was further replaced by the present Albert Bridge in 1871, so named in memory of Queen Victoria's husband Prince Albert. On the abutments on the face of the bridge are placed painted bronze medallions of Queen Victoria and Prince Albert which add a touch of brightness and festive effect to the appearance of the work-a-day bridge. On the inner facing of both the east and west parapets at the southern end of the Albert Bridge are clearly chiselled, on the polished Peterhead granite blocks, the following inscriptions:

ALBERT BRIDGE
ERECTED BY THE TRUSTEES OF GLASGOW BRIDGE
ACT OF PARLIAMENT PASSED AD 1866
THE HONOURABLE JOHN BLACKIE JUN. LORD PROVOST

ALBERT BRIDGE
COMMENCED A.D. 1868
THE HONOURABLE JAMES LUMSDEN LORD PROVOST

Similarly, on the parapets at the northern end of the bridge are:

ALBERT BRIDGE
THE FOUNDATION STONE LAID 1870 BY THE
EARL OF DALHOUSE GRAND MASTER MASON OF SCOTLAND
THE HONOURABLE RAE ARTHUR LORD PROVOST

ALBERT BRIDGE
OPENED A.D. 1871
THE HONOURABLE WILLIAM RAE ARTHUR LORD PROVOST

In 1730, in common with many other villages around Glasgow, Gorbals began to develop as a weaving centre and thrived until the advent of the spinning mills which threw many out of work. When it was annexed in 1846, it could be said that Gorbals was Glasgow's first industrial expansion area south of the River Clyde. Prior to this the Scottish parliament passed an Act in 1661 giving the Magistrates and Council of Glasgow the power to select Baillies for Gorbals. This method of administration was continued until 1846. As far back as 1285, Gorbals was known as Bridgend due to its proximity to the old bridge over the Clyde. Later in the early seven-

Glasgow Bridge & ford, 1720

teenth century it took its new name from the surrounding Barony of Gorbals. When the Barony of Gorbals was bought by Glasgow in 1647, it included the districts of Kingston, Tradeston, Laurieston and Hutchesontown and extended south to Strathbungo. At the present time Gorbals comprises the districts of Laurieston/Gorbals and Hutchesontown/Gorbals.

The Hutchesontown area of Gorbals was acquired by the brothers George and Thomas Hutcheson of Lambhill, who also instituted a hospital and school. A building at 158 Ingram Street, known as the Hutchesontown Hospital, was founded by them. Two large statues of the brothers adorn the facade of the building

At the beginning of the seventeenth century it was the aim of John Laurie, son of a wealthy timber merchant of Jamaica Street, to turn Gorbals into a showpiece suburb of Glasgow. He succeeded extremely well and built the well-known thoroughfares now known as Warwick, Salisbury, Portland, Oxford, Norfolk, Cumberland, Cavendish and Bedford Streets. Carlton Place and Bridge Street, which was originally called Bloomsbury Street, are attributed to him. The houses built by Laurie in the district of Laurieston stood the test of time for well over a hundred years and it was hard to believe that they would eventually become slum property.

The Townland

Main Street, 1800s

A good deal of conjecture is current regarding the derivation of the name Gorbals. Gorbals is an ancient expression in Scottish law meaning tiends, or from the gaelic words 'gor' meaning a piece of land or territory and 'baile' meaning a town or village. Together the words mean townland, and therefore the name Gorbaile became corrupted through usage into Gorbals, a feasible explanation due to the district's association with Glasgow.

Gorbals does not possess a coat of arms and what is sometimes erroneously accepted as the coat of arms is in reality the arms of Viscount Belhaven (Robert Douglas) who owned the lands of Gorbals in 1634. A letter received by an interested party from the Court of the Lord Lyon confirms that it is the Douglas coat of arms and not the arms of Gorbals and reads as follows:

I have made a search in the register and confirm that no arms were recorded in the public register for the burgh of Gorbals. It appears that the seal is the coat of arms of James, Marquis of Douglas, but like many arms used in burghs in these days were made without authority.

> Court of the Lord Lyon
> H.M. Register House
> Edinburgh 1969

The seal referred to in the letter is a treasured possession of Mr. Charles Edmiston Douglas, City Auctioneer, and is of silver with the coat of arms of Douglas as verified by the letter. It was used to stamp official documents and was in use from 1710 till 1846. The dominant feature of the seal is the emblem of the heart of Bruce, an association with Sir James Douglas who was killed by the Moors in battle in Spain while taking the heart of Bruce to the Holy Land. Before Douglas was killed he threw the casket containing the heart well in front of him and uttered the well-known stanza: 'Forward as thou inert wont, noble heart; Douglas will follow thee or die'.

It is interesting to note that Mr. C. Edmiston Douglas's great grandfather, Mr. Andrew Gemmell, was the last Chief Magistrate of Gorbals (he was sometimes referred to as the last provost of Gorbals) before it was annexed to Glasgow. Consequently Mr. Douglas possesses many relics of old Gorbals including a bible dated 1814 which states in the fly leaf the following information: 'When attending church officially prior to November 1846 at which date Gorbals was with other suburban burghs amalgamated by act of parliament with the city of Glasgow and constituted one grand municipality and this bible with relative psalm book was on 9th November 1858 presented by the then Lord Provost and magistrates of Glasgow to Mr. Andrew Gemmell, writer, who was the last chief magistrate of Gorbals who has been a city councillor for upwards of 11 years and who has been elected one of the magistrates of said city and I the said Andrew Gemmell do hereby leave and bequeath the relict of the old constitution of Gorbals to be preserved by my only son Andrew and his heirs as an heirloom in the family. Glasgow 15th November 1858.'

Mr. C. Edmiston Douglas also has in his possession a testimonial from the Cotton Spinners of Glasgow in gratitude for his great grandfather's defence of five of their members who were accused of murdering John Smith on 22nd June 1837. Smith was a cotton spinner employed in Houldsworth Mill, Anderston, Glasgow, and the incident took place while he was walking along Clyde Street. Smith was probably considered a blackleg by the men Mr. Gemmell defended. They were found not guilty of murder but were transported beyond the seas for seven years.

Many of the old and familiar landmarks of Gorbals which are dear to the hearts of Gorbolians are fast disappearing. Decay and change are seen all around. Neglected and dilapidated buildings are razed to the ground and concrete buildings gradually rise in their place. But let us have a look at some of the most noteworthy buildings before they disappear from the Gorbals scene for ever.

The Citizens' Theatre, Gorbals Street was founded in 1943. On the wall of the foyer is a plaque, to the memory of the founder, which was unveiled by J. B. Priestley in 1956.

On the opposite side of the foyer is a similar plaque to Richard Waldon, the English owner of the Princess's Theatre (founded in 1866) which was the forerunner of the Citizens' Theatre. It reads:

THIS THEATRE
CAME INTO POSSESSION OF
RICHARD WALDON
1886
DIRECTED AND MANAGED BY
HIM UNTIL HIS DEATH IN 1922

Richard Waldon and his Scots successor Harry McKelvie were responsible for turning Glasgow pantomime into world beating entertainment and featured such well-known artists as Tommy Lorne and George West. The last pantomime to be shown in the Princess's Theatre was 'Hi Johnnie Cope'. It is interesting to note that Richard Waldon worked under Sam Bough, the artist and painter, whose paintings are on display at Kelvingrove and the People's Palace Museums, Glasgow. The foyer also displays a metal statuette in memory of the late well-known actor Duncan MacRae.

The six statues which ornament the top of the Citizens' Theatre have long been a question of conjecture as to whom they represent but it is believed they symbolise the following characters. Facing the Citizens' Theatre, from the right, is the figure of Robert Burns next to a lady holding a lyre, possibly representing music. Continuing in line is a dancer, a figure of drama holding a mask, another lady possibly representing literature, and lastly Shakespeare. The architect of the figures was a Mr. Douglas and they were sculptured by the hammer and chisel of Mr. John Mossman. The neighbouring Palace Theatre was built in 1904 and is now a bingo hall.

At 144 Gorbals Street is the Gorbals Corporation Swimming Baths, the oldest in the South side of Glasgow, and built in 1885. They were originally known as the South Side Baths, and according to the visitors' book the baths were visited in 1921 by the Chief Engineer, City Planning, of Osaka, Japan, and his remarks are written in Japanese. Although the signatures are not too easily read, it appears to be signed S. Motinyama. In 1914 M. Yoshimura, Tokio, Japan, also paid a visit.

David Crabbe, the well-known swimming instructor, who trained Nancy Riach and Cathie Gibson, at one time gave diving displays in the swimming pool. It was also frequented by the Police training college personnel including the late Willie Burns who, from 1927–1931, won 20 Scottish championships varying from 50 yards to

880 yards. In the vestibule of the baths is a plaque in memory of 17 members of the South Side Amateur Swimming Club who fell in the first Great War. This club was formed in 1879 and probably was the first organised in the South side of Glasgow. Among the members were swimmers of championship class including Jeana McGuffie, Scottish Junior and Senior champion 1936–37, Hector Faller, Scottish graceful diving champion for five successive years 1923–28, Mamie Lamont, Scottish graceful swimming champion 1928–29, and Effie Lobban who won the Gantocks Clyde Swim three times. The ladies of the club held the Glasgow Corporation team race trophy for 17 years, 1922–38.

Gorbals John Knox Parish Church at 34–36 Carlton Place was built in 1806–10. The spire at one time was struck by lightning and badly damaged. The architect was David Hamilton, grandfather of Madeline Smith of the famous 19th century murder trial. It is probably the only church in Gorbals to hold gaelic services.

Gorbals Street School

Farther along, at 22 Carlton Place, is the gateway to Gorbals Primary School built in 1884. Perusing through the school attendance book of 1885, it was discovered that more than half the pupils were Jewish giving rise to the fact that Gorbals was the first home of the Jews in Scotland.

In the stone above the doorway leading to the playground is cut the unusual symbol of a beehive. Appropriately enough the beehive and the bees symbolise work and obedience, diligence and eloquence, creative ability and wealth. Strange to say, the emblem of the beehive was accepted as a tradition among Moslems and many of their children are now pupils at Gorbals Primary School. It is intended that the beehive stone will be saved when in 1972 the school and John Knox church will be demolished to make way for the new Sheriff Court Buildings. Adjacent to Gorbals Primary School is Buchan Street where stands the building of the old Gorbals Police Barracks. The street was then known as Albion Place and this fact is clearly seen cut on the stonework of the building.

Farther east in Carlton Place, at Nos. 51–52, is one of the oldest notable buildings in Gorbals. Laurieston House, built in 1802–4 by the architect Peter Nicholson, is a fine example of the type of house built by Laurie the builder of the district of Laurieston. The interior plaster work is of exceptional quality. It is now inhabited by the Corporation of Glasgow Health and Welfare Department and will be retained. The old Gorbals fire station at 128 Nicholson Street is a shadow of its former glory and silently awaits the push of the bulldozer to demolish it into nothingness. A relic of the fire station, the old fire drum, is on show in the People's Palace Museum.

In South Portland Street is the Great Central Synagogue. Inside the premises are two plaques which state:

TO THE NEW CENTRAL SYNAGOGUE
DANIEL ROSENBLOOM ESQU.
FOUNDER PRESIDENT
1925

CONSECRATED BY J. H. HERTZ   OPENING FUNCTION
CHIEF RABBI   MAURICE BLOCH
JUNE 1925   JUNE 1925

and MERGED WITH THE GREAT SYNAGOGUE 17th Feb. 1956.

The adjacent Jewish Institute was opened by Isaac Woolfson and cut in a stone at the entrance is this information

THE INSTITUTE WAS OPENED BY
ISAAC WOOLFSON ESQU.
23rd June 1935   22 SIVAN 5695

Hutchesons Boys' Grammar School was originally in Ingram Street where initially 12 boys received free education. In 1840 the school was transferred and rebuilt at Crown Street, Gorbals. It was demolished in 1969.

Churches & Buildings

John Knox Church

The former Hutchesontown Church of Scotland (at Caledonian Road), built in 1856-7, has a magnificent tower and is considered one of Glasgow's outstanding nineteenth century buildings. Unfortunately it was badly damaged by fire and the exquisitely designed roof and interior destroyed, but in spite of this the building was ultimately preserved. St. Francis's Roman Catholic Church in Cumberland Street is the largest church in Gorbals and was built by the Greyfriars who were the founders of the old Greyfriars Monastery which at one time stood on a site opposite the *Daily Express* building in Albion Street, Glasgow. During 1969-70 the church authorities spent £60,000 renovating this well designed church which was built in 1868. Renwick United Free Church, Cumberland Street, was built in 1869 and named after James Renwick the famous covenanter who, in 1688, aged 26, was the last covenanter in Scotland to be martyred on the scaffold at the Grassmarket of Edinburgh. In 1941 this church was united with the closed down Laurieston church, Norfolk Street. The combined church is now known as Laurieston-Renwick Church of Scotland, Cumberland Street. It may be of interest to know that a Diamond Jubilee service, held in the church in 1913 and lasting 2¼ hours, had no fewer than 12 ministers and two lay preachers taking part.

Chalmers Church at 100 Pollokshaws Road was built in 1897 and was united with the closed Abbotsford Parish Church, Devon Street, in 1933. The united church is now known as Abbotsford Chalmers Church. The old Abbotsford church was reputed to have had the second largest church bell in Glasgow. The two brass war memorials of the united churches are placed on the wall on each side of the pulpit. What arouses one's interest on observing the memorials is the fact that in the 1914–18 war 518 members served in the forces and of this total 72 were killed in action. At that time the congregation probably numbered around 2,000 compared to the present day figure of about 380.

It is reputed that the only landmine dropped in Gorbals during a raid in the 1939 war destroyed the interior of St. Margaret's and St. Mungo's Episcopal Church, Rutherglen Road. It has since been rebuilt, and the church is the proud possessor of a 150 year old organ which is of very high quality and is on occasions borrowed by the Glasgow University Choir.

Perhaps one of the oldest picture houses in Glasgow was the Wellington Palace situated in Commercial Road now demolished to make way for the new housing development. Adjacent to the cinema was left standing, apparently for ornamentation purposes, a red granite fountain which is now surrounded by tall new buildings, and occupying a site in the middle of Waddell Court. Reading the inscription we find it was gifted by Alexander Lamberton in 1899. A metal plate, which apparently gave much fuller information about the donor, appears to have been wrenched away by vandals. Taking time to examine the history of the donor, it was discovered that he was Managing Director of John Gray & Co. Ltd., Confectioners, Adelphi Terrace, and that he was interested in the well-being of the community and in the temperance cause. Strangely enough, while gathering data in the Southern Necropolis, Caledonia Road, the name Hugh Lamberton, a merchant of Glasgow who died in 1888, was noticed chiselled on a large handsome tombstone. It transpired upon further research that he was a brother of Alexander Lamberton, born in Portugal Street, who was also a Managing Director of John Gray and Co. Ltd. and the Scottish Cold Storage Co. Ltd. and a director of the Dunoon Convalescent Homes.

Gorbals like many other districts of Glasgow in the past had a large percentage of 'single-end' houses which produced gross overcrowding. In order to overcome this problem, the Sanitary Department instituted 'ticketed' houses which meant that a small plaque was fixed to each door stipulating the number of adults therein. For instance, $3\frac{1}{2}$ inscribed on the plaque meant 3 adults and 1 child only were permitted to live in the house. Fortunately this method is no longer required. At the rear of the close at 80 Nicholson Street is situated a unique two storied building with an outside stairway. It is literally built on the back court and is known as a back loan house. This method of building simply added to overcrowding and insanitary conditions.

Gorbals was densely populated and had no parks and very few trees. The residents could, however, cross the Suspension Bridge over the Clyde at McNeill Street and take advantage of the fresh air and beautiful rural setting of Glasgow's oldest park, the Glasgow Green. At the present time there is an Adventure Playground at Lawmoor Street, Gorbals. It is the first of its kind in Scotland and provides a wide variety of interests for children. It was opened in 1964 and will eventually form the nucleus of a Little Neighbourhood Park which will comprise 19½ acres.

The Hutchesontown Gardens were first opened on a site at

Back Loan House

Crown Street in 1835 with the primary purpose of providing a healthy recreation and diversion in the form of growing fruit, flowers and vegetables. This met with great success, but due to the building expansion in Gorbals, the gardens were shifted in 1866 to a 7½ acre site at Butterbiggins Road. The gardens were removed in 1876 to a site of 8¾ acres where Prince Edward Street, Crosshill, now stands. There are two plaques mounted on the building at the corner of Prince Edward Street and Niddrie Road to this effect. Ultimately in 1892 the gardens were re-established at Shawmoss Road, Crossmyloof, only to be discontinued in 1965.

For about 200 years before 1958 the most notable landmark in

Gorbals was Dixon's Ironworks, better known as Dixon's Blazes, and so called because the huge flames rising from the chimney stacks cast a lurid glare throughout the area. William Dixon, the founder, was born in Newcastle-on-Tyne in 1753, and became the largest mine owner in Scotland. One of his mines was the little Govan Colliery in the Gorbals. Dixon died in 1822, and Dixon's Blazes was taken over by Colvilles' Steel Works in 1958 and demolished in 1960.

Arising from the dust of the demolished buildings in Gorbals are many new schools carrying on the tradition of education which the Hutcheson Brothers started in the sixteenth century and which resulted in the famous Hutchesons Boys' Grammar School being built in Gorbals. The new Adelphi Secondary School, 20 Commercial Road, was opened in 1967 superseding the old Adelphi Terrace School at Florence Street, which now serves as a centre for the Glasgow College of Building and Decorating for Apprentices. On a wall in the interior of the Adelphi Secondary School is a plaque which states: 'Corporation of Glasgow. Adelphi Secondary School. This School was formally opened on Tuesday 31st January 1967 by Councillor George H. Moore, J.P., Convener of the Education Committee.'

Robert Burns' works are kept alive in Gorbals by the efforts of the Thistle Burns Club which offers prizes to the pupils of Adelphi School for the best rendering of the poems and songs of the national bard. It is of interest to note that the Blind Burn flows underneath the Adelphi Terrace School. It has its source near the Queen's Park main gates at Victoria Road and forms the eastern boundary of the old Parish of Gorbals. While workmen were digging the foundations of the New Adelphi Secondary School what was thought to be secret underground passages were discovered, and it was surmised that they led to Elphinstone Mansion at one time situated in Gorbals Street.

Blackfriars Primary School, at 310 Cumberland Street, was opened on Tuesday 6th February 1968 by Councillor John J. McCrossan, J.P. This school derives its name from the old Black-friars Monastery which once stood off High Street, on the site of the College Goods station opposite Blackfriars Street, Glasgow. The school stands on the old Parliamentary constituency of Blackfriars and Hutchesontown which was created in 1885 and then in 1918 was split up and renamed. George Buchanan, M.P. for Gorbals from 1922–48, was born in Gorbals in 1890 and died in 1955. He was known as one of the wild men from the Clydeside and attended Camden Street School, 305 Florence Street, which is now lying derelict. He instituted the Buchanan Memorial prize for good citizenship awarded to any child attending this school. This prize was transferred to Blackfriars School which now replaces Camden Street School.

St. Bonaventure was a Franciscan monk born in Tidanza, in the Province of Tuscany, Italy, in 1221, and it is his name which is perpetuated at St. Bonaventure Secondary School which was opened in 1939 and stands in the Parish of St. Francis. On the banks of the River Clyde at Crown Street has been built, appropriately, the Glasgow College of Nautical Studies, which has been acclaimed worthy to win a Civic Trust award for architectural design from 25 entries. It was opened by Lord Mountbatten and boasts a boat house on the river, a Planetarium which was the first to be built in Scotland, and an observatory on the roof. A plaque on the wall of the assembly room states: 'This College was officially opened by Admiral of the Fleet The Earl Mountbatten of Burma K.G. P.C. G.C.B. O.M. D.S.O. F.R.S. 4th October 1969.' At present there are 1,000 students on the roll and the college is visited by many organisations.

The face of Gorbals is changing fast and the traditional stone built four storied tenement is rapidly disappearing with tall steel and concrete multi-flats and maisonettes taking their place. At Caledonian Road, Adelphi Street and Rutherglen Road these spectacular buildings, appearing to break the sky line, can be seen. In 1961 Queen Elizabeth visited the flats at Rutherglen Road, which is now known as Queen Elizabeth Square in her honour, and a plaque fixed to a wall states: 'Queen Elizabeth Square. This commemoration stone was unveiled by Her Majesty Queen Elizabeth on occasion of her visit here. 30th June 1961.'

In the middle nineteenth century Gorbals had a big influx of Jewish people followed by the Irish. In the 1890s, Glasgow was one of the main cities of opportunity in Europe.

More recently there has been an invasion of Pakistanis and Hindus and in 1963 there were reputed to be 10,000 of them in Gorbals. At the present there are only around 600, most having moved to other areas due to redevelopment of the area. A young Muslims' League (Y.M.L.) was formed in 1968 which has its own magazine called *The Young Muslims,* and a centre has been provided at 27 Oxford Street where they can participate in a wide variety of sport. The membership at present is 100. The Muslims plan to built a handsome Mosque of Islamic architectural design costing £150,000. It is to be situated in Adelphi Street and one day in 1975 its graceful minaret will cast a reflection on the bonnie waters of the River Clyde.

Notabilities

Thomas Lipton

Gorbals has always had the reputation of being a fighting quarter and this is true in vastly different ways. During the depression of the '30s, many gangs came into being and they adopted colourful names often associated with their area or street. The South Side Stickers, the Cumbies from Cumberland Street, the Coburg Erin from Coburg Street and the Beehives. Strangely enough, they usually confined the fighting to their own ranks and seldom molested outsiders. On the credit side, and according to Duke Metcalfe the boxing promoter, Gorbals was the most famous nursery in Scotland for producing sportsmen, especially boxers and footballers, and on an examination of this statement it is found to be more than true. Benny Lynch, the flyweight boxer, was Scotland's first Champion of the World. He was born in 1913 at 17 Florence Street, which is now demolished, and began his training in a hall attached to St. John's Church, Portugal Street. Benny died a pauper in 1946. It is has also been said that Johnnie McGrory, featherweight champion of Great Britain 1936-7, was a Gorbals man. Jim Campbell, Scottish flyweight champion, was born in Cumberland Street. Elky Clark, another ring hero, lived in Mathieson Street, and John (Cowboy) McCormack, yet another boxing star, lived in Florence Street, Gorbals. Billy Paddon, flyweight, was born in South Portland Street, and the district produced two great footballers, Pat Crerand, born in Thistle Street, and Charlie Gallacher who hailed from Cumberland Street.

Probably the oldest living sportsman to come out of Gorbals is 86 year old Dan Flynn who was born in Crown Street. In the year 1905 he was Amateur Middle Weight Champion of Scotland. In

1911 he beat Dixie Kid who in that same year had beaten George Carpentier, later to become Heavyweight Champion of Europe in 1912. Flynn, a great all-rounder, was heavyweight champion of Scotland in 1912 and in 1904–5 became champion cyclist of Scotland and also held the British and Empire Championship for six years. He competed in the Olympic Games at Crystal Palace, London, and was also a swimmer of ability, one of his feats being to swim across the Holy Loch. Numbered among Flynn's friends was Victor McLaglan, the American film star. To this day Dan Flynn has fond memories of Gorbals and the friendly atmosphere which prevailed during his memorable sporting days.

Sir Thomas Lipton, who became the prince of British grocers and also a millionaire, was born in Crown Street, Gorbals. His frequent attempts to win the Yachting Trophy, the America Cup, were unsuccessful, and many of his trophies are on view in the People's Palace Museum. Lipton left his million pound estate to the city of Glasgow. Kennedy Jones, the Australian editor and multi-millionaire, was born in the same Gorbals close as Lipton, and living across the landing from Sir Thomas were the brothers R. and J. Dick, nicknamed 'Gutta Percha' Dick. They were the pioneers of the multiple shoe shops and their shoes sold for 5/- a pair in 1870.

It was a man from Gorbals, Allan Pinkerton, who founded the world famous detective agency in America. He was born in Muirhead Street (also known as Warm Water Street) in 1819 and the Pinkerton Detective Agency was started in 1850. It could be said that his agency helped to tame the 'wild and woolly west' and greatly subdued the Mafia. At one period Pinkerton was the only detective in Chicago and on one occasion acted as bodyguard to Abraham Lincoln.

Walter Wilson was born in Main Street, Gorbals, in 1849, and in the year 1869 he founded his hat cleaning and blocking business in the Colosseum, Jamaica Street. He named the firm Walter Wilson & Co. Ltd. In 1901 Wilson took over the McLellan Galleries (which had been vacated, its art collection transferred to the New Art Galleries in Kelvingrove Park) and the well known firm of 'Tréron et Cie' was born. Dr. George Mathieson, the theologian, was born at 39 Abbotsford Place in 1842. Blindness struck him when he was 19 years of age, and during his ministry of Innellan Church he was known as the 'blind minister', composing the hymn which made him famous 'O love that wilt not let me go'.

More and more names liken themselves to Gorbals. John Anderson, founder of Anderson's Polytechnic, Argyle Street (now Lewis's Polytechnic) opened his first shop in Clyde Terrace,

Gorbals, in 1837. John Buchan, 1875–1940, who was 1st Baron Tweedsmuir, famous Scottish author and Governor General of Canada, wrote over 50 books, including *39 Steps* and *Greenmantle*. His father was minister of John Knox Church at the corner of Bedford Street and Surrey Street where Lipton's Garage now stands. Sir Isaac Woolfson was born in Thistle Street, and as their birthplace Gorbals can proudly claim Sir Alexander Fleck Baron, British industrialist, Lord Traynor the lawyer, and Lord McGowan.

William Simpson, R.I., otherwise known as 'Crimean' Simpson, was born in Anderston in the last century and has many fine water colours of old Gorbals on display at the People's Palace. Included among them are one of Buchan Street showing John Knox Church and Carlton Place, and another of the Elphinstone Tower, Main Street, Gorbals.

The derivation of many of the streets in Gorbals gives one a clue to the local history. For instance, Hospital Street is named after St. Ninian's Hospital which was founded by Lady Lochow in the year 1350. The railway running parallel to Eglinton Street was at one time the bed of the Paisley and Johnstone Canal which had a Port Eglinton at this point. The port and adjacent street were named after the Earl of Eglinton. Adelphi means, in Greek, two brothers, and Adelphi Street was opened at the beginning of the nineteenth century in memory of the Hutcheson brothers. Waddell Street was built on the Stonefield Estate and called after the proprietor Mr. Waddell. Gorbals has the distinction of possessing the shortest street in Glasgow. It is Langbank Street, which is 30 feet long, and runs off Eglinton Street.

Before Gorbals became an industrial area, it was, in common with other districts in the Clyde valley, covered with beautiful estates. For example, between Butterbiggins Road and Gushetfaulds, lay Larkfield Estate, after which Larkfield Corporation Transport Depot is named. It is said that the last person to live in the now demolished Larkfield Mansion was a Mr. Barr who was manager of Dixon's Blazes. Illustrated on a map of the Barony of the Gorbals (reproduced on previous page) is Butterbiggins Estate which lends its name to Butterbiggins Road. There are also the lands of Gallow Know, Bryce Land, and Gushet Faulds, and it is noted that Inglefield Street perpetuates the name of the Inglefield Estate. A consortium of railways eventually took over this area, covering the land with a vast network of steel rails, consisting of the oldest railway on the south side of Glasgow namely the Pollok and Govan railway 1830 which had earlier been used by William Dixon for transporting coal from his Little Govan coal pits to the River Clyde, the Glasgow Southern Terminal Railway 1846 which

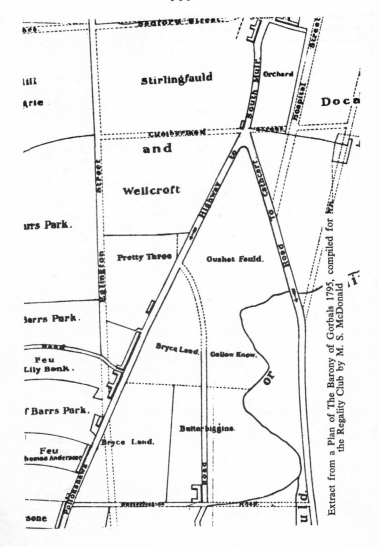

Extract from a Plan of The Barony of Gorbals 1795, compiled for the Regality Club by M. S. McDonald

joined the Glasgow City Union Railway 1864 and the Caledonian Railway 1873. The lovely tree lined estates rapidly disappeared to make way for such businesses as the Strathclyde Distillery, Adelphi Street and the Co-op bakery. Their first loaf of bread was baked in 1869 in a small Scotch oven in a bakehouse at 50 Coburg Street on a site where the Coliseum now stands. In McNeill Street, in 1887, the U.C.B.S. opened a large bakery which was then called the Garden bakery. It was reported that 30,000 people attended the opening of the bakery which could have supplied all Glasgow with bread.

Gorbals Burial Ground at Rutherglen Road was opened in 1770 and many who died in the cholera-epidemics of 1832 and 1848 are buried here. In recent years the burial ground has been made into a rest park and the tombstones have apparently disappeared except for a few which are situated against the boundary wall. Four remaining tombstones have the insignia of the old time trades sculptured on their stone faces. Three of them are dated 1723 and the other 1741. John Wilson, a friend of Robert Burns, who represented Wilson in his poem 'The death of Doctor Hornbook', is buried here, and a stone is erected to John's memory with an inscription stating this fact. Unfortunately the inscription plate has been destroyed by vandals. It is also reputed that a man who was hanged for stealing a sheep was buried in the Gorbals graveyard.

The Southern Necropolis burying ground in Caledonia Road, originally a part of the Estate of Little Govan, was bought by a joint Stock Company around 1840. Many well-known citizens of Gorbals and other districts are buried in this cemetery. A fine polished granite stone marks the last resting place (lair 3791) of Sir Thomas Johnston Lipton, K.C.V.O., who died 2nd October 1931, and who is buried with his family in a tomb much visited by American tourists. In the central portion of the cemetery is a granite stone with a metal plaque with the features of John Robertson embossed upon its surface and an inscription which clearly states: 'This monument erected in 1912 by members of the Institution of Engineers and Shipbuilders in Scotland to the memory of John Robertson, Engineer, born 10 December 1782, died 19 November 1868, maker of the engine of the Comet, 1872, the first steamboat that plied regular in Europe'. A few yards away is a memorial to Hugh McDonald, author of *Rambles round Glasgow* and *Days at the Coast*. He lies buried beneath a small white granite stone in the form of a scroll which is pleasantly shaded by a Chinese dwarf willow. The inscription simply reads: 'Hugh McDonald, Poet, Born 4th April 1817 died 16th March 1860'. A tombstone situated against the wall to the left of the main gateway brings back shades of Sir Walter Scott. It is stated thereon: 'Rev. Nathaniel Paterson, D.D. a grandson of Scott's Old Mortality and the author of the Manse Garden born in the Parish of Kells, Kirkcudbright 1787. Died at Helensburgh 1871.' A metal plaque of his face adorns the tombstone. An interesting stone was discovered in the cemetery which states: 'In loving memory of George Halket M.D., F.R.F.P.S.C., one of the founders of the Royal Samaritan Hospital who died the 6th October 1928 aged 79 also his wife Helen Harkness died 5th February 1959 and 97 years'. Upon investigation, it was found that a picture hanging on the wall of the board room in the Royal Samaritan Hospital, Victoria Road, was of the original Samaritan Hospital which stood in South Cumberland Street from 1886–1890. This is probably the hospital with which the above mentioned Dr. George Halket was associated.

Among the silent ranks of tombstones there is one to the memory of Rev. James Smith, M.A., which states that he was the author of the *Divine Drama of History and Civilization* and *Moral and Religious Essays of the Family Herald*. Till his death in 1857, aged 55 years, the Rev. James Smith was popularly known as 'Shepherd' Smith, no doubt after a paper called the *Shepherd* which he edited in 1834. He was also considered a prophet and expounded a doctrine of his own which, in these days, might have been described as mystical universalism. Half a million people read his weekly essays for the *Family Herald* which were unique in so much that the *Herald* was the first specimen of a periodical to be produced entirely by machining types with paper and printing. The weekly issue was priced one penny. Smith was also responsible for editing the *Crisis* for Robert Owen the Socialist.

Perhaps the most unusual tombstone in the Southern Necropolis is that in the form of an arched freestone block mounted with a huge vase. On the face of the stone is inscribed the words: 'A few friends have placed this vase over the grave of William Robb born 1816, died April 1845'. It has been said by modern monumental sculpturers that this stone would probably cost in the region of £3,000 if made today, but when the stone was first cut to shape it cost only a few pounds because at that time sculpturers received only a penny an hour.

But the story of Gorbals rolls on, her great contributions to the world far outweighing her liabilities. She appears, in this the bi-centenary of the parish, to be ever striving to live up to her ancient motto SANS TACHE which in French means 'without spot or blemish'.

Bridgeton

When one walks through the parliamentary division of Bridgeton situated in the east end of Glasgow which embraces Calton, Dalmarnoch, Camlachie and part of Mileend you are struck by the general scene of decay and neglect that pervades the area. Street after street of tall tenements stand stark and empty, their shattered windows lying open and gaping to the sky. Broken glass lies in profusion on the streets and in the interior of the empty houses vandals have been busy stripping lead from the pipes of the water supply and the unchecked running water floods the derelict houses. Of late flourishing engineering works, mills and factories have been closed down and transfered elsewhere leaving Bridgeton with the appearance of a ghost town.

Although a poet might find very little at the present time to inspire him to write verse about Bridgeton, nevertheless, it has its distinction. It possesses the largest Burns Club in the world founded 1870 and comprising some 1,400 members. Burns visited the Saracen Head Inn, Gallowgate, Bridgeton, in 1788, and Wardsworth the famous English poet in 1803. But Bridgeton had her own local poet Alex Rodger, born 1784 - 1846 also weaver and music teacher who composed the well known song 'The Muckin' O' Geordies Byre."

Saracen Head Inn was built in 1754 from stones taken from the demolished Bishops Palace which stood adjacent to the Glasgow Cathedral. The Saracen Head Inn was the terminus for the stage coach from London which took about 12 days to travel the 400 miles from London to Glasgow but in 1836 the mail coach arrived at the Saracen Head Inn from London in the record time of 42 hours. The Saracen Head was the rendezvous of the elite of the city where many splendid functions were held , something of its past grandeur can be seen in the form of a five gallon punch bowl on show at the Peoples Palace, Glasgow Green, with the words inscribed on the inside of the bowl SUCCESS TO THE TOWN OF GLASGOW. The site of the Saracen Head Inn is now occupied by the Saracen Head Public House which still exhibits a few relics of these times.

It is interesting to note, that the Bridgeton Burns Club in 1874 initiated competition among the local schools for the best rendering of the works of Robert Burns, in the form of solo and choir singing and recitations.

Bridgeton was the home of many of the well known Glasgow gangs such as the Billy Boys, The Norman Conks, The Dale Street Boys, The Redskins, and The Baltic Fleet. Tradition dies hard in Bridgeton and many of the old slogans of these former gangs can be readily seen scrawled on the walls throughout this highly congested area, but strange to say Bridgeton was also the home of a late Chief Constable of Glasgow, Walter Docherty, who was born in "St Helena", a cottage situated behind Main Street, Bridgeton. When Richard Widmark, the famous American film actor, visited Bridgeton in May, 1961, he stated that the place was worse than Chicago, at least that was Chicago's opinion, Razors, Bicycle chains, Billy Boys even heard of them. However Widmark had a certain affinity to Scotland, his grandmother Mary Barr hailed from Kirkcudbright and he claims she was the prime mover in his decision to become a film star.

But in spite of what has been said Bridgeton has a tremendous amount to be proud of. Bridgeton was the stamping ground for many budding men of industry in the early pioneering days of Glasgow and many great names have been fostered and kept alive as a result.

Not least was James Maxton, known as the beloved rebel, who was born at Pollokshaws 1885. He was elected M.P. for Bridgeton in 1922. For a period he was a teacher in St. James Primary School, No. 88, Green Street, Bridgeton. The school is proud to display a plaque to his memory on the wall of the interior of the school.

As already stated Bridgeton was one of the early industrial meccas of Glasgow. As far back as 1785 David Dale and George MacIntosh established the first Turkey Red Dying Works in Britain at Bridgeton. George MacIntosh invented the India Rubber Macintosh. David Dale built mills at New Lanark in 1785 that became one of the display pieces of Europe and his advanced ideas on social reform were ahead of his time. David Dale was buried in

Ramshorn Churchyard, Ingram Street. The David Dale College at 161 Broad Street, and also Dale Street, Bridgeton are named after him.

In the early nineteenth century there were many weavers in Bridgeton and in 1787 during a riot to oppose the reduction of their wages three were killed and several injured, they were buried in the Abercrombie Street graveyard where a large inscribed memorial stone giving a brief history of their fate can be seen. In the same graveyard lie the Mortal remains of Abraham Lincoln's minister which states simply on the much photographed tombstone thus

Rev. James Smith D.D.

Son of Peter and Margaret Smith

Was born at Glasgow May 11 A.D. 1798

Minister of the Gospel for forty years

In the

United States of America

In his declining years he was appointed

U.S. Consul at Dundee

By Abraham Lincoln

Whose Pastor he had been

And where he departed this life

July 3rd a.d. 1871

A Sinner Saved By Grace

Many of the epitaphs on the existing tombstones of this ancient graveyard are grim and searching by modern standards for instance written on a tombstone date 1780 are the words:

Gone as a sound

All flesh is born to die

Surviving friends

Come view the ground

Where shortly you must ly

Another stark warning is depicted on the tombstone of Robert Shaw, Calton, 1806, it bluntly stated Remember Death. On another adjacent stone is marked the pungent word — THIS

Probably the oldest person to be buried in this graveyard was in 1928 namely Agnes Murdock who died at 106 years of age. The Abercrombie Street graveyard was first opened by Calton Corporation of Weavers in 1786.

Before Bridgeton was annexed to Glasgow in 1846 it was a beautiful residential area consisting of a few country estates. Bridgeton was originally known as Barrowfield as it was built principly on the estate of Barrowfield but when the Rutherglen Bridge was built over the Clyde in 1775 it was renamed BRIGTON later Bridgeton in honour of this event.

Calton which was originally known as Blackfaulds (meaning fold of black cattle) was a town with its own police force when Bridgeton was a small village without a police force, this encouraged roughs from Calton to come into Bridgeton and engage in street fights while the Calton Police watched them unable to intervene as they were in Bridgeton and outside their control. Calton was anxious to take over Bridgeton but in 1846 they were both annexed to Glasgow and ironically Calton is now part of Bridgeton.

The Bridgeton Umbrella is a famous landmark elegantly built

The Umbrella, early 1900s

of cast iron and rising to a height of 50 feet it was executed and designed by Messrs. George Smith and Company of the Sun Foundry. The Camlachie Burn flows underneath close by the umbrella its pristine glory gone and now reduced to the status of a common sewer, although in its hey day delicious silver eels were fished by the basketfuls from its crystal waters.

Clementina Walkinshaw the youngest daughter of the 3rd Laird of Walkinshaw was associated with Bonnie Prince Charlie when he was stationed in Glasgow during the Jacobite Rebellion in 1745. She accompanied the prince when he later went to France. They had a daughter named Albany. Burns wrote a poem in praise of their daughter entitled the "Bonnie Lass of Albany" the first stanza thus:—

> My heart is wae, and unco wae
> To think upon the raging sea
> That roars between her gardens green
> And the Bonnie Lass of Albany.

Albany Street in Bridgeton is named after her.

Clementina Walkinshaw spent part of her early childhood at Camlachie Mansion that is situated near General Wolfe's Public House, Gallowgate. Due to the Laird of Walkinshaws adherence to the Jacobite cause his estates were forfeited and latterly John Orr acquired the estates and he carried on the work of developing the expanding village of Bridgeton which his predecessor had started.

In 1749 Lord George Sackvilles regiment commanded by Lieutenant Colonel Wolfe, of Quebec fame, arrived in Bridgeton. At this period there were no army barracks in Glasgow so it fell to the lot of John Orr to quarter Wolfe in Camlackie Mansion which he owned. Wolfe visited John Orr frequently at his resident mansion of Barrowfield.

Due to Napoleon's threat to invade these shores the infantry barracks adjacent to Barrach Street, off Gallowgate, were built in 1795 and were later demolished in 1877. They were later superceded by the newly built Maryhill Barracks which in turn have been demolished in recent years.

The son of John Orr of Barrowfield who carried the same name and title became the principle town clerk of Glasgow, a much coveted post as it is on record that an official tried to bribe the Provost by offering him £1,000 for the post of Town Clerk. A plaque can be read in the Glasgow Cathedral in honour of his memory.

St. Mary's R.C. Church, Bridgeton, was opened in 1842 and is the oldest R.C. Church in Bridgeton and the second oldest in Glasgow. The Celtic Football Club was founded in 1888 in St. Mary's Halls, Orr Street, by Marist brother Walfrid. Initially the primary function of forming the football club was to raise funds to provide meals for necessitous children in the east end of Glasgow. The first sermon preached in St. Mary's was by the Rev. Theobald Mathew born near Cashel Tipperary in 1790. He was a pioneer in the temperance movement in the R.C. Church. The temperance movement was started in Ireland in 1838 when William Martin, a Quaker, appealed repeatedly to Rev. Mathew to start this movement in order to cut down the prevalent drunkenness among all classes in Ireland.

Last tram procession, Bridgeton Cross

At 182, Main Street, Bridgeton, was the site of the Swan Tavern and Tea Garden, it had the first Zoo in Glasgow in 1830 people flocked from the surrounding district to view the animals and sit under the trees and eat curds and cream. Only one tree was left standing in the black court of 182 but in 1963 it was cut down and now only the stump remains.

What may be considered the oldest house in Bridgeton is situated at 332, Crownpoint Road. It was originally the Crownpoint Mansion built in 1761 by William Alexander and was named after the well known stronghold on the Canadian frontier which was captured from the French by General Amhurst. Up till recently it was the offices of the British Basket and Besto Company Ltd.

Charlotte Street leads to the Glasgow Green through a splendid entrance, the original entrance to the Athenæum in Ingram Street. Charlotte Street was built in 1779 an area previously known as Merkdaily which means a daily market where vegetables and fruit could be bought. Many famous men were associated with Charlotte Street. David Dale the Philanthropist and industrialist built a town house here in 1782 at a cost of £6,000, it was demolished a number of years ago to make way for an extension of Our Lady and St. Francis School annexe. In this house his daughter was married to Robert Owen who was latterly the manager of the New Lanark Mills.

John Gibson Lockhart, the famous author who was married to Sir Walter Scott's daughter Sophia in 1820, died in No. 40 Charlotte Street, now demolished, Thomas Campbell, poet author, of Lord Ullin's daughter lived here while compiling "Pleasures of Hope." John Stuart Blackie, lecturer and poet, was born here, Alexander Smith also lived here, he composed a poem "Glasgow". Dr. Thomas Chalmers, Scottish divine born 1790, author of Problems of Poverty, resided here for a while. Thomas Carlyle, the historian, visited Dr. Chalmers when he lived in Charlotte Street.

Allans Pen caused a great deal of controversy in the past and is still remembered by the people of Bridgeton, the site of Allans Pen is at the junction of Newhall Street and Green Head Street. Mr. Allan, Sugar Trader and Manufacturer, owner of Newhall Mansion built a pen or tunnel to give him easy access from his nome to the river Clyde, unfortunately in doing so he infringed the public rights of the people who became so incensed that they boycotted the work which he gave them to do, even though he offered them increased payment. The corporation here placed a plaque on the wall at this site which simply states "Allans Pen."

In Tullis Street, adjacent to the picturesque Glasgow Workers Dwellings now scheduled for demolition, is an ancient derelict graveyard, the headstones are broken and the epitaphs mainly unreadable. It was opened in 1871 and closed in 1876 and was thought to have been associated with the Bridgeton Relief Church.

The most impressive tombstone remaining has been smashed by vandals but with some effort it is still readable and the wording tells a tragedy of long ago.

In looking back at the Glasgow Courier, Saturday, December 6th, 1856, an account is given of this fire. It states that the fire took place in a large warehouse at 74 Buchanan Street and 23, Exchange Square. The premises were occupied by Messrs. Ewing Paul & Co., Messrs. James Black & Co., Messrs. Oswald Stevenson & Co. and Mr. Cowburgh. They were engaged in silk, muslin and yarn trades. Damage was estimated at £100,000 and stated to be the most destructive fire for many years.

To the sporting fans of Glasgow. The Scottish National Olympic Club in Olympia Street, Bridgeton, now closed, must raise nostalgic memories, it was the scene of many a hard boxing bout, such notable boxers as Peter Keenan, Dick Calderwood, Dado Marino and Jim Higgins trod the canvas in this once popular arena.

The old early nineteenth century tollhouse at 556, Dalmarnoch Road is reminiscent of the time when transport was slower and more leisurely than at present. The toll was collected here for Rutherglen and it cost a penny. It is said that it is the only building in Glasgow with a chimney directly above the main door. Christ Church Episcapal, Church Brook Street, was built in 1835. Cannon John McBain born 1909 who ministered in this church was the first clergyman to become a Baillie in the Glasgow Town Council. Many of the soldiers from the old Infantry Barracks, Gallowgate, attended worship in this Church.

The Greenhead and Barrowfield Parish Church, built 1850, at

570, London Road is the first church of Scotland since the re-formation to have murals installed in the church. Seven murals depict the creation of man. It took Alisdair Grey the painter three and a half years to complete this work. This church has also the distinction of possessing the only full timbered hammer beam roof in Scotland which was gifted by the Tullis family, who were leather Merchants. Tullis Street was named after them.

James Templeton & Company Ltd., carpet manufacturers, Templeton Street, Bridgeton, is a long established firm, James Templeton the founder was born in Campeltown 1802. He first started in business at Paisley making Paisley Shawls in 1829, eight years later the trade in Paisley shawls declined and then he turned his attention to making chenille carpets and consequently assured future success in the manufacture of carpets.

Templeton Carpet Factory fronts on to the Glasgow Green and according to the stipulation of the corporation all buildings fac-ing the green must present a pleasing appearance. It is said that Mr. Templeton tendered to the corporation three designs, they were all turned down. He then turned to his Architèct and asked him what was the finest building in the world, "The Doges Palace" he replied, so a design of the replica of the Doges Palace was sub-mitted to the Corporation, it was readily accepted and the present building was built in 1857 to the design of the Doges Palace.

John Lyle a weaver from Kilbarchan was the first foreman em-ployed in Templetons Carpet Factory. After 14 years' service he left to set up in business for himself as a carpet manufacturer. The premises are still at No. 10 Fordneuk Street and were founded in 1853.

Maver and Coulson, Electrical Engineers, have their head-quarters in Bridgeton. It was founded in 1883 and employs about 1600 people in their Scottish factories. They pioneered the develop-ment of coal cutting machines.

It is worth while mentioning the once famous Argyle metor car factory which was opened in Hazier Street, Bridgeton, in 1900, and closed in 1927. It was one of the first and biggest motor car fac-tories in Europe. Three of the Argyle cars are at present on show at the Glasgow Transport Museum, Albert Road. Two. are 1900 models and the other one is a 1907 model.

The Peoples Palace Museum, Glasgow Green, depicts many pictures of old Bridgeton, also a portrait of David Dale, the industrialist, and Frederic Lamond pianist and composer. A baton belonging to the old Calton Police Force can be seen in a show case.

Glasgow Green, 1700

Other note-worthy people who were associated with Bridgeton was Hugh MacDonald, author of Rambles Round, Glasgow, and Days at the Coast. He was born in Romford Street in 1877. Fred Lamond, 1868-1948, was appointed organist of Newhall Parish Church, Bridgeton, at the age of 10. He later became a famous British concert pianist. Myer Galpern born 1903, Lord Provost of Glasgow 1958-60, M.P. for Shettleston 1959. David Ewart. portrait painter.

The last two mentioned were known to be pupils of John Street Public School, Bridgeton.

The sacred heart primary school, 31 Reid Street, Bridgeton, is an ultra modern building with hexagonal classrooms. It is said that it is the only school in Scotland with sand blasted murals executed on the external walls. The work was done by William Mitchell from London.

Bridgeton slowly rises anew from the rubble and perhaps an inscription aptly inscribed above the archway inside the working men's club. Laudressy Street, Bridgeton, would be a fitting inspiration to Bridgeton's future.

LEARN FROM THE PAST
USE WELL THE FUTURE

Characters

The Cast-Iron Tombstone

Sighthill, Springburn, is so called because from its summit can be seen a superb panoramic view of the surrounding district. It is perhaps the best known hill in Springburn due, no doubt, to the fact that successive generations of Glaswegians lie sleeping in this hallowed spot. Sighthill Cemetery, of some 48 acres, crowns the crest of the hill, was opened by a joint stock company in 1840 and is now cared for by the Glasgow Corporation. When it was opened it was considered one of the most beautiful and tastefully designed areas in the city. From its near 300 ft. height could be seen on a clear day 13 portions of the neighbouring counties framed by the contours of Ben Lomond, Ben Ledi to the north, Goatfell in Arran and the dark outline of the Argyllshire mountains to the west. Of course, today the view is somewhat obscured due to the presence of high buildings erected in recent years.

Sighthill Cemetery's first officially recorded interment was on 24th April 1840 but, strangely enough, there is a stone in the cemetery dated 1834. Since then, however, many handsome and well designed stones have been erected and still retain an element of beauty in spite of the ravages of time, wind, rain and sun, not to mention the destructive hands of vandals who, with careless irresponsible action and lacking of respect for law and order or even the dead, have knocked down and smashed hundreds of stones in this 'city of the dead'. Some of the best sculptured and noteworthy tombstones were erected by J. & G Mossman, the Master Sculptors, who still carry on business at 56 Cathedral Street, and who were established in 1816. Many of the early Mossman family were interred in the cemetery. The firm was responsible for sculpturing such well known works as the monument to Burns' Highland Mary in Greenock, half of the statues in Georges Square, Glasgow, and the massive figures which adorned the frontage of the St. Andrew's Halls, Glasgow. St. Andrew's Halls, destroyed by fire, is now being rebuilt and fortunately these figures will be retained in a much needed extension to the adjacent Mitchell Library.

While wandering through the confines of Sighthill Cemetery, gazing with melancholy sadness at the inscriptions, the memorial stones, in many cases, tell simple stories of the aspirations and successes of the silent tenants lying beneath. On reflection it seems hard to believe that the dust they are now, once breathed the full breath of life and that they were then a power in the land. Many led a life of good works, ever mindful of the welfare of their fellow man. We now enjoy the result of their efforts and the fruits of their labours are taken for granted. Such was one's thoughts when confronted by a tombstone with a sculptured head on its surface. It simply read.

This Stone
is placed over the grave of
John Milne Donald
Landscape Painter
by a few friends
and admirers of his genius
born at Nairn in 1817
died at Glasgow July 1866
also
Tom William Donald artist
his only son
died 21st January 1883 aged 29 yrs

Researching into the life of John Milne Donald, it was discovered that he was one of the foremost Landscape Painters in the West of Scotland and associated himself with art circles in the city. He was a member of the once West of Scotland Academy and exhibited his pictures at their annual shows. He also contributed to the fair started by the Glasgow Institute of Fine Arts.

Another stone overlooking the Sighthill multi storied flats catches our attention for here lies the remains of the first member and janitor of the Grove Street Home Mission Institute. The obituary gives a brief history.

Grove Street Home Mission Institute is situated at the corner of Grove Street and Balnain Street, Cowcaddens. It was built in 1865 and founded by Wakefield MacGill in 1859. Inscribed on a stone, high on the face of the building, are the words 'Bear ye one another's burdens' and the Institute has certainly lived up to this well known Bible text. It played a great part in the religious life of early Glasgow including the ministering of medical aid to the poor long before the benefits of the Health Insurance Act came into force in 1911. It has, up to the present time, maintained its grand tradition and its influence has been spread abroad but, sadly, this fine building will soon be demolished.

Many notable people of different shades of opinion are interred here, and the most widely visited last resting place is that of the martyrs John Baird and Andrew Hardie, who were weavers by trade, and suffered death at the time of the Radical rising in 1820. Some distance away is situated a simple white granite tombstone in the shape of an Iona cross, and at one time a metal violin aptly adorned it before being removed by vandals. The reason for the violin can be readily understood when the well cut inscription is read.

Homage
to the memory of
W. Mackenzie Murdoch
violinist and musical composer
born at Glasgow 28th July 1870
died 18th April 1923
The most renowned interpreter
of the
Soul of Scotland's music in his day
erected by admirers whom he charmed
by the magic of his bow
unveiled by Sir Harry Lauder 25th September 1924

At the beginning of Mackenzie Murdoch's career he was closely associated with Sir Harry Lauder and travelled widely with him on concert tours. He composed the well known 'Hame O' Mine', and violin solos 'Culloden, Waverley, Glencoe and Among the Heather', and was one of the founders of the Scottish Musical Artists' Benevolent Association. Murdoch died in Lennoxtown but his home was at 270 Great Western Road, Glasgow.

Many of the memorials give brief and concise histories in their lettered passages and the obituary to James Haldane is equally informative of a philanthropist of the city.

James Haldane Esquire
Born 1782 died 2nd April 1866
Engraver in Glasgow
whose love of art
and desire to promote
the prosperity of his fellow
citizens induced him
to devote his fortune
to the foundation of an academy
for the cultivation of
the fine arts
in Glasgow

We leave this tombstone of the great benefactor, and we make our way to a large low-set red granite monument which covers the remains of one of Glasgow's great founders of the shipbuilding and engineering industry. Robert Curle was a Troon shipbuilder who joined Robert Barclay's shipbuilding business in 1840 when Barclay controlled three shipbuilding berths and two repairing berths at Stobcross, Glasgow. As we wend our way along the cemetery lanes we notice two more tombstones to shipbuilders, namely Robert Henderson and James McArthur. Both men, no doubt, also helped to make the Clyde the foremost shipbuilding centre of the world.

Situated beside the main avenue leading up to the circular path at the summit of the cemetery stands a large white tombstone which commemorates the Rev. James Aitcheson Johnston, who died in 1895 at Mosesfield House, Springburn. He was for 34 years minister of Johnston Church in Springburn, so called in honour of him. He was the father of George Johnston who helped to change the mode of travel in this country by designing the first British motor car, and he was the founder of the Arrol Johnston car firm whose first car was put on the market in 1895. Several of these solidly built beautifully finished Arrol Johnston cars are on show at the Transport Museum, Albert Avenue, Glasgow.

Perhaps the most unusual memorial stone in the cemetery can be seen situated near the circular path. It is made entirely of cast iron and a casual assessment of its weight would be in the region of 40 or 50 tons. It is intricately designed in the shape of a church with two ornate spires and the name Forrest is engraved on the iron memorial without any other apparent information.

Roman Springburn

Dinosaur's Egg?

Passing through the present day Springburn, it would be hard to believe that the district was ever at any time associated with the ancient Empire of Rome, that empire which flourished for 500 years (27 B.C.–476 A.D.) and which brought about great changes, advances and civilisation to the then World.

Indeed Springburn was part of that Great Empire and it lay only a few miles south of the Antonine Wall which was the most north-westerly Roman outpost. The wall stretched for 37 miles across the waist of Scotland with forts positioned at two mile intervals along its entire length. Lollius Urbicus, the Roman Governor of Britain, undertook to build the wall and named it in honour of the ruling Roman Emperor Antoninius Pius (86–161 A.D.) who had never set foot in Scotland. It was built specifically to serve as a bulwark against the wild Picts (the Romans renamed them the Caledonians) who inhabited the country on the north side of the wall and whom the Romans were unable to subdue. Springburn then would be forced into the unhappy position of playing the part of a buffer district due to its proximity to the frontier. Especially so when the Caledonians engaged in their many frequent assaults against the Romans, and when they broke triumphantly over the wall Springburn must have suffered the terrors of armed invasion. It is sure that many Springburn men were conscripted into the Roman forces and shipped abroad to help defend the German frontiers, their sojourn there being verified by inscribed records on memorial stones to the men of old Scotland.

In Petershill Lands, Springburn, Roman coins were unearthed several of which were minted in the reign of Emperor Commodus, who was considered such a poor ruler that he was killed by his soldiers. A single large brass coin depicts Commodus's wife Crispina, whose beautiful grecian features are clearly marked, and some indication of the style and rank of ladies of these Roman times can be seen by observing this well preserved coin. Despite her beauty and apparent charm Commodus put his wife to death. It is thought that Roman soldiers may have dropped these coins during a skirmish when they perhaps ventured forth boldly from the safety of the nearby Roman forts of Kirkintilloch and Cadder which were situated on the Antonine wall.

Peculiarly enough, Springburn still retains a lasting link with Rome which proudly boasts her seven hills. Springburn can, with equal pride, also point to seven hills within her confines: Balgray-hill, Barnhill, Keppochhill, Petershill, Sighthill, Springburnhill and Stobhill.

The Antonine wall was built in 140–142 A.D. and the Roman road which led to it at this point passed through Springburn and roughly followed the line of the modern Springburn Road finally terminating at the Roman fort at Cadder. The south end of this road joined the main east and west Roman road which passed through Drygate, Glasgow. It must have been stirring times in these far off days when the Roman Legionaries of the 2nd, 6th and 20th Legions (the three legions which took part in the building of the Antonine wall) freely used this road through Springburn trans-porting supplies, men and equipment. They would make their way through wild and rugged terrain, the hills or Drumlins, bristling with ancient moss covered trees, and the low lying ground between the hills pitted with treacherous bog and deep marshes. Formid-able wild life abounded in the shelter of the woods bordering the road including the Scottish brown bear, wolf and wildcat. The Roman soldiers were ever on the alert for the sudden attacks from such animals, and the even more dangerous unnerving guerrilla tactics of the Springburnians who, no doubt, would be anxious to expel them from the occupied country. It is possible that Agricola, the Roman Governor of Britain 78–86 A.D., used this road when he advanced into Scotland in 80 A.D. in an endeavour to subdue the inhabitants.

At the close of the second century, however, the Antonine wall was abandoned by the Romans and they withdrew their forces to the south and stationed themselves along the 73 mile length of the Hadrian wall which stretched from the Solway to the River Tyne. In all probability the men of Springburn would join forces with their brothers north of the Antonine wall and jointly drive the Romans out of Springburn and Scotland to this second line of defence.

Some interesting exhibits of the Roman period can be seen at the old Kirk Museum, Kirkintilloch. At the north-west corner of the Peel Park, Kirkintilloch, excavations have laid bare the stone foundations of the Antonine wall. The Hunterian museum at Glasgow University has on view a selection of Roman antiquities from Cadder and Kirkintilloch and the coins found at Springburn.

A good example of a 20th Legioh stone tablet found at Cadder is:

> IMP CAESAR 1
> T AELIO HADRI
> ANO ANTONINO
> AVG PIO P P
> VEXILLATIO
> LEG XX VAL VIC F
> PER MIL PIII

A Vexillation of the 20th Legion the Valerian and Victorious (did the work of the Vallam) for 3,000 paces (a roman pace equalled 5 of our linear feet).

It is interesting to note that the Caledonian Railway Works, Springburn Road, perpetuates the ancient Roman name of Caledonia for the world famous locomotive works which is now sadly defunct.

In 1900, during quarrying on the site of the New Albert School extension in Mansel Street, Springburn, what was thought to be a fossilized egg was discovered. It is now in the safe custody of the Springburn Association and is perhaps the only existing tangible record of the Springburn primaeval animal life period. It leaves one to conjecture the point as to whether the embryo is one of the seven or eight species which at one time or another frequented the Clyde Estuary. For example, the barnacle goose, the grey lag goose and the pink footed goose. Recently the Springburn Association sent the egg to the Glasgow University to be analysed. A zoologist, geologist and archaeologist found it a very interesting discovery but they did not want to commit themselves as to its type. It was stated by one of them that there was a remote chance of its being a Dinosaur's egg. If the egg had been left in its natural strata, it might have proved a priceless find.

Alpine Springburn

Glasgow from north east, 1692

Due to the irregular topography of Springburn it is sometimes referred to as the Alpine district of Glasgow or the Highlands of Glasgow. This feature has given rise to an abundance of burns or streams and a number of lochs, but through the passage of time the lochs have been drained and the burns buried. According to a map, edited by Sir James Marwick, LL.D., and dated 1650, Petershill Loch is the only one shown and has since been drained. It lay in the vicinity of Flemington Street just on the north border of the Petershill F.C. ground. A burn flowed from this loch and served as a tributary of the Garngad Burn and merged with its waters at the site of the old Germiston Works, Petershill Road.

From the springs around Pinkston rose the Pinkston Burn and it made its way under the Cowcaddens and New City Road where it joined the Woodside Burn and then tumbled into the river Kelvin in the area of the old Hillhead Ford at Woodside. In the 1830s the water of the Pinkston Burn was noted for its purity and was freely used for bleaching purposes.

The Garngad or Gad Burn which made its way right through Springburn had its source in a spring on the uplands of High Balornock Farm near the Mansion House of that name, from whence it tumbled down the grassy slopes and entered the grounds of Forrest Hall hospital. Following the line of Darnick Street, it meandered through the grounds of the now defunct Braby's Works where it caused much flooding. Finally it joined the Molendinar Burn at Alexandria Parade. This burn gave its name to the old district of Garngad, through which it flowed, and is now known by the new name of Royston.

Possil Burn had its birth at the foot of Balgrayhill and fought its way parallel with Elmvale Street through the district of Possil and finally joined the river Kelvin.

St. Roch's Loch was situated at the juncture of Parliamentary Road and Castle Street and its waters fed the St. Enoch or Glasgow Burn, which flowed gently down the slopes through Cowcaddens, the west side of Buchanan Street, struggled beneath West Nile Street and Mitchell Street before entering the Clyde near Jamaica Bridge.

An interesting reminder of this burn came to light during the demolition of an old building situated between Buchanan and Mitchell Streets. When the paving stones were removed in the back-court, a sixty foot length of well constructed conduit was discovered which at one time had served the purpose of carrying the waters of the St. Enoch Burn. It was quite dry but the bottom was covered with layers of sand.

The boating and duck pond in Springburn Park drains itself into the Knock Burn which flowed in a northernly direction. Rob-royston Loch, which was situated in the north-east corner of Springburn, has been drained and it was the source of the tributaries which fed the Knock Burn.

The Broomfield or Germiston Burn was a tributary of the Garngad Burn and had its beginning in the area north of St. Philomena's Primary School, Robroyston Road. This was quite near the site of the former Provanmill Dam and it joined the Garngad Burn at the junction of Petershill Road and Red Road.

This area, so richly endowed with a wealth of watering places, was aptly called Springburn, and it takes its name from a burn, long since forgotten, but thought to be the original Spring Burn which found its life at a spot quite near Balgray Tower at Broomfield Road. From there, it splashed down the slopes and joined the burn flowing from Petershill Loch which was a tributary of the Garngad Burn.

The rugged, hilly contours of the countryside formed many rain catchments and fostered many tributaries which in turn fed the burns already mentioned. These tributaries have been mistakenly thought by the laymen to be the main burn, but this error is understandable as the names of the tributaries have been forgotten and apparently never recorded for posterity.

In the middle of the nineteenth century industrialisation came swiftly to Springburn. Railroads, factories, warehouses and mills were speedily built and coal and iron mines came into being. The vast earth excavations required for this transformation soon played havoc with the natural topography of the district and the burns, which had graced the area from the beginning of time, and which had served the inhabitants faithfully for hundreds of years, were ruthlessly and ignominiously buried underground in ducts and used as foul sewers which carried the refuse from the industry which now abounded in the area.

Houses and streets were built upon the catchment areas and the rain, which once fed the burns, was now drained into the sewers. The bogs and marshes have also been drained, and sadly the once pleasant burns and streams are now lost.

A typical case in point is that of the Garngad Burn, which is no longer a tributary of Glasgow's sacred Molendinar, but which is now reduced to a sewer which flows into the main drainage of the Dalmarnock Sewage Works.

At a meeting of a committee, held in Glasgow on 12th May 1857, on sanitary improvements, the interim report describing the condition of the Pinkston Burn which passed down 2,000,000 gallons of water daily, is given below.

'The colour of the water passing thro' the burn is constantly changing and ranges from milk-white to ink-black and occasionally red, green and yellow, being receptacle for the waste and refuse of a variety of chemical manufacturers, distillers and dyers etc., so that its composition is constantly varying. The smell coming from the water also differs both in intensity and kind and seems a mixture of all abominations altogether indescribable and the temperature of the water being generally from 70 to 90 degrees F, the gases are mixed with watery vapour producing a most sickening and disease predisposing effect.'

So now the burns of Springburn have passed away from the eyes of man, and no longer will the sparkling, singing streams which danced down the steep braes between rocky banks carpeted with broom and heather and masses of swaying bluebells, ever again afford the subject of a pleasant country walk in a long summer evening. No longer will youngsters, ever bent on birdnesting, search the leafy branches of the elm, oak and silver birches which once cast their long shadows on the crystal clear waters, where the salmon, trout and silver eel swam in constant awareness of the fisherman's rod. Nor hear again the sudden shot from the gun that heralds the capture of a plump pheasant and which temporarily silenced the sweet singing of the thrush, the lark and the linnet.

The coming of the dark, satanic mills and workshops which have since polluted the air with smoke and fouled the streams with chemicals is always regretted although we recognise that the manufacturers provide the work and wages necessary for the life of the people. But, it has been a doubtful exchange.

The Rev. R. L. Telfer, one time minister of Ferguson Memorial Congregational Church in Palermo Street (now known as the Calvary Tabernacle), states that a burn flows through the basement

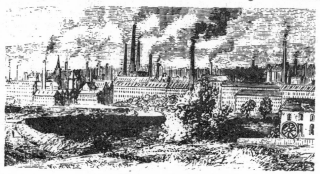

Glasgow from east, 1814

of the church. It would appear that the burn, ever fearful of degenerating to a sewer like its unfortunate confrères, has sought sanctuary in the depths of the church. It is said that its waters look pure and untainted, and perhaps even now it is not too late to resurrect this burn and use it for ornamental purposes. Another burn which has a penchant for the church is reputed to have its source beneath the foundations of Springburn Parish Church in Hillkirk Street.

It may be worth noting that the Wellfield Street multi-storied flats are built on the site of Wellfield House. A drinking well existed here of which, it has been said, 'Caused no small amount of trouble during the building of the flats due to the presence of irrepressible water'. The overflow from this well is thought to have formed the Wellfield Burn which probably flowed into the Garngad Burn.

There was also said to be a well, situated on vacant ground, the one time property of William Little & Co., in Southloch Street, which also had an overflow burn, and again a tributary of the Garngad Burn.

Springburn was amply provided with a good supply of drinking water as is quite clearly evidenced by the names given to the thoroughfares. There is Adamswell Street, Fountainwell Road, Springvale Terrace, Wallacewell Road and Wellfield Street. In days of yore, Springburn must have been a very beautiful place before her hills and dells were taken over for the needs of industry.

20,000,000 gallons of water, emanating from the Mingavie Water Works, flow beneath Springburn Road each day to help to supply Glasgow with one fifth of her total water supply. The water is carried in 2 cast iron pipes, each 36in. in diameter, and the route is via Balmore Road, Hawthorn Street and Springburn Road into the centre of Glasgow. At Coburg Place, the two pipes are concealed in the high elevation of High Springburn Road which runs parallel with Low Springburn Road. One of the water-pipes was laid on the 14th October 1859 to carry water from newly-opened Loch Katrine via the container locks at Milngavie, while the other pipes were laid in 1900.

Springburn has many reminders of pre-Reformation days and not least is Saint Roche or Saint Rollox Chapel and Cemetery which stood at Castle Street near the site of the present St. Rollox Church of Scotland at the corner of Springburn Road and Fountainwell Road. It derives the name from Roche or Roque, who was born in Montpellier, France, in 1295 of a very rich family. When born, he had a large red birthmark on his side in the shape of a cross. He served in a hospital at Aquapendente in North Italy during the plague which swept the Continent, and it is said he performed wonderful cures by making the sign of the cross on the foreheads of his patients. He was canonised and is known as the patron saint of the sick. The present church of St. Roche, Royston Road, was built in 1907 and is said to be the only Roman Catholic church in Britain to be so named. St. Rollox Co-operative Society and the district of St. Rollox also perpetuate his name.

Bishops House, a pre-Reformation edifice which stood in Bagnall Street, off Broomfield Road, was reputed to have been a country house of the Bishops of Glasgow before 1560, and it is said that this was the first house in Scotland to hold Mass after the Reformation. There is a Piscina inserted in the garden wall of the former Sight-hill Manse at 23 Broomfield Road. The Piscina was in use in pre-Reformation days, and is a deep, sandstone basin, used by the priest for cleansing purposes after the Mass had been celebrated. It is not yet known where it originated, but perhaps it was salvaged from the old, pre-Reformation church of St. Roche. Also, adjacent to the Bishops' House, stood old Mosesfield House which was considered

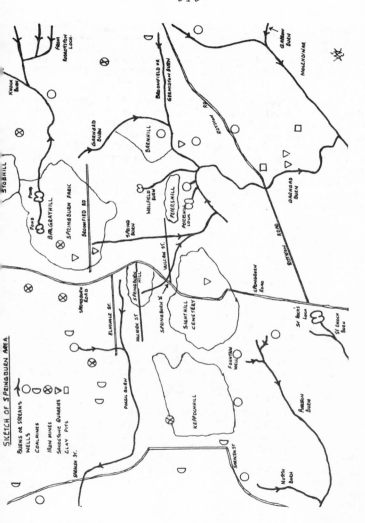

SKETCH OF SPRINGBURN AREA

to be of great antiquity. The Rev. J. Prendergast, minister of Sighthill Church of Scotland, saved two portions of ornamental pillars from this building during demolition and these are perhaps the only surviving link with this ancient building. They now help to ornament the garden of his home at 38 Cornhill Street, Springburn.

Who was Brother William? Until quite recently, an observant passenger travelling by train over the Cowlairs Incline adjacent to Sighthill Housing Scheme might have noticed a memorial stone.

Enquiries revealed that the stone was erroneously called the Martyr's Stone in memory of a victim who died of the plague when it visited Glasgow in 1647. During the construction of the Edinburgh and Glasgow Railway in 1839 it was found necessary to remove the stone and it was built into the side of one of a number of cottages nearby. They were afterwards called the Martyr's Cottages. The cottages were later removed and the stone was placed permanently beside the track. During construction work on the Sighthill Development Scheme it was accidently smashed and it is hoped someone will replace this historic monument.

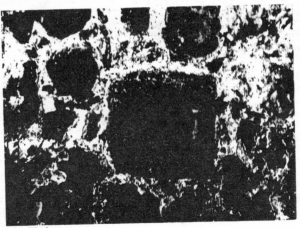

The Piscina

Local Hills

SPRINGBURN PARK

Rob Roy, the famous Scottish Outlaw, and a number of his men were passing down what is now known as Springburn Road on their way to visit Bailie Nicol Jarvie in Glasgow. Darkness gradually descended upon them and Rob Roy, anxious to obtain shelter, was delighted when he perceived through the gathering gloom the twinkle of lights from an inn. The inn was situated at what is now the corner of Fountainwell Road and Springburn Road. 'Come Lodge My Loons', shouted Rob Roy to his followers who speedily took advantage of the timely hospitality and the inviting cabaret. History records that, thereafter, this inn became known as LODGE MY LOONS and became a popular rendezvous and well-known landmark until it was demolished early in the last century. Bonnie Prince Charlie is also reputed to have stayed there in 1746.

In the second half of the 18th century, Industry began to develop in Springburn. Coal was extracted from the ground to feed the hungry furnaces of the foundries and factories, and sand pits and quarries were opened up to help build viaducts, houses and roads. The Monkland Canal was built in 1793, at a cost of £120,000, in order to bring more coal from the collieries of Monkland in North Lanarkshire, and was to become the most profitable canal in Scotland. It has been said that the money obtained from the forfeited property of the clan chiefs after Culloden helped build the Forth and Clyde canal which was also used largely for the shipment of coal. It was opened in 1790 and cost £330,000. Both canals brought great prosperity to Springburn.

Perhaps the best way to describe Springburn is to illustrate the present day features of the separate hills within its confines.

STOBHILL is the highest hill in Springburn and it is appropriate that the largest acute general teaching Hospital in Scotland should be situated on its summit. According to Dr. Oliver M. Watt, Senior Consultant Anaesthetist, Stobhill Hospital, until recently, was the largest hospital in the United Kingdom and is unique in many respects. It stands on a superb site on the highest part of Glasgow. It has ample room for expansion and is the only hospital to contain within its walls a large Victorian mansion, Belmont House, which in 1936 was bequeathed to the Corporation of Glasgow by Sir Hugh Reid on the understanding that it would be used as the Marion Reid (nee Bell) Home for Children, in memory of his wife. From the windows of Belmont can be seen seven counties. Recently a new operating theatre suite was opened and cost over half a million pounds. It is by far the most up to date and modern theatre suite in the United Kingdom.

BELMONT HOUSE

Belmont House was in its day the largest mansion house in Glasgow and was the home of Hugh Reid, son of James Reid, who played an important part in the early years of the steam locomotive industry in Springburn. It was built in 1889 and appears to have had two further extensions added in 1899 and 1905. A very fine sundial ornaments the building. The Reid family presented the Glasgow Art Galleries with a number of rare pictures of great value including a Constable, a Corot and a Turner in addition to a very fine oil painting of James Reid which can be seen there to this day.

Situated in the north-east corner of Stobhill Gardens is a pets private cemetery which at one time belonged to the Reid family. Three iron plaques with the names of pets still exist. There were five plaques but two of them were vandalised.

BALGRAYHILL is 351 feet above sea level and a panoramic view of the countryside can be seen from it. Commanding the crown of the hill is Springburn Park, which is dominated by a water reservoir, 80 feet above ground level, containing 2,000,000 gallons. The park was formerly known as the Mosesfield and Cockmuir estates. The original Mosesfield Estate was bought by William Moses who made a fortune in hiring Sedan chairs in Glasgow. He bought this estate, comprising 100 acres, and gave it his own name. Springburn Park was acquired in 1892 and parts added in 1900 and 1904. Hugh Reid of Belmont gifted part of the lands of Cockmuir and also the New Mansion of Mosesfield and grounds. At present Springburn Park covers 78 acres. Fittingly situated in a prominent position in the park is a monument to James Reid who, in his time, was leading world-wide pioneer in steam locomotion. The Reid family were extremely generous to the people of Springburn in their efforts to help to beautify Springburn Park. They gifted £10,000 to build the winter gardens which contain the largest single glass house in Scotland and which was opened in 1900. The bandstand was an additional gift. In the centre of the park stands a beautiful column with a unicorn mounted on top of it. On the four sides of the column are portrayed the coats of arms of Scotland, England, Ireland and Glasgow. This column, which was also a Reid gift, was shifted from the children's Pleasure Ground a few years ago to its present site for safe keeping and protection from vandals.

Balgray Tower, a well-known landmark and popularly known as Breezes Tower, is a Tudor single-storey house with a three storied centre octagonal tower built in 1830 and is situated at 50–52 Broomfield Road. It is perhaps the most unique building in Springburn. At 140–142 Balgray-hill Road stands a two storied semi-detached villa block with semi-octagonal bay windows. This building was designed by the famous architect C. R. MacKintosh and was built in 1890. Until quite recently there hung on the wall of the Springburn bowling green a sketch of Geordie Stewart's Inn which in the middle of last century stood at the foot of Balgrayhill. It had a ring attached to the wall where farmers tethered their horses while they were having a refreshment. This sketch has unfortunately disappeared.

SPRINGBURNHILL is the hill most closely associated with the original hamlet of Springburn which came into prominence in the middle of the nineteenth century. It lay to the north of the village which was situated at the corner of Cowlairs Road and Springburn Road and cut on the stonework at the top of the corner tenement is the inscription SPRINGBURN CROSS 1886. Springburn village is reputed to have taken its name from the Spring Burn which flowed in close proximity. The burn has now virtually disappeared.

Springburn North Hill Parish Church in Hillkirk Street is the oldest church in Springburn and was built in 1842. It was originally known as Springburnhill Parish Church before it was amalgamated in 1967 with Springburn North Church which stood for 78 years at the corner of Elmvale Street and Springburn Road. Unfortunately it was burned down in 1968, a deed thought to have been the work of vandals.

PETERSHILL was the site of Petershill Mansion which was built about 1760 and designed by John Adam, the architect. Little trace remains of this mansion except perhaps the main doorway, which has a unique mason's mark, and which was re-erected as an ornamental archway in the garden of Bedlay Castle, Chryston. John Stobo, a Glasgow merchant, who resided at Petershill Mansion, was responsible for draining Petershill Loch which was situated on the south side of Petershill. The Petershill Junior Football Club was opened in 1935 by Lord Provost Swan and the opening event was a friendly match between Rangers and Celtic watched by 28,000 spectators. It has been said that the site of the old loch, which was until recently the property of farmer Paddy Orr, proved an excellent football pitch. This worthwhile club has a plaque on the outside wall to the memory of one of the founders. It reads: 1905–1945 George Henry Memorial President of Petershill F.C. Vice-President of Scottish Junior Football Association 1942–1945. This Tablet Has Been Erected To His Memory As a Token Of Respect By His Many Friends In The Football World.

BARNHILL gave its name to the poorhouse which was built there in 1853. In the year 1810 a mental asylum had been built in Parliament Road and in 1843 was transferred to its present site at Gartnavel. The vacated building in Parliamentary Road was, in the same year, taken over as the city poorhouse which in turn was transferred and amalgamated with Barnhill Poorhouse in 1905. Strict discipline was observed in Barnhill. Able bodied inmates were required to make up 350 bundles of firewood per day and stonebreakers were expected to break up 5 cwt. of whin metal per day. Any inmate not producing the stated amount was put on a bread and water diet in solitary confinement for 12 hours. Disorderly conduct such as swearing or breaking of rules, resulted in being put on a diet, excluding milk and buttermilk, for a period of three days. In 1945 Barnhill was renamed Foresthall House and Hospital, and the place can be aptly described as a village within a city. It occupies 33¹/₃ acres of great natural beauty. Wide, well attended lawns add a fine setting to the rowan, laburnum, hawthorn and sorbus trees and their blossoms in season, mingled with the snowdrops, crocuses and daffodils, add an intricate pattern of colour against the green background of the lawns. The grey lines of the buildings speak of an age of Victorian grandeur although they have a slightly military appearance. The gardens are maintained by a staff of nine employed by the Parks Department. Near the paint shop is a well, covered by a manhole, which is 60 feet deep and which served the Poorhouse with water in days gone by. Foresthall has undergone many improvements within recent years and a plaque on the wall of the sitting room indicates this fact. It has been suggested that Foresthall be abandoned and the site used for industrial development. It would be more in keeping with the traditions of Springburn if this tastefully landscaped area was kept if only as an illustration of the improvements which can be made, by the efforts of the Springburn people, in transforming a Poorhouse into a beautifully designed hospital.

Industrial Springburn

On Keppochhill is situated Cowlairs Park which was opened in 1920 and consists of 35 acres which include a modern football pavilion and nine football pitches. In the days before commerce and industry came to Springburn there were many fine mansions set in beautiful country estates within the confines of the district. Cowlairs Mansion, built in 1824, once stood in Cowlairs Park, and it was on Cowlairs Estate that Michael Scott, author of *Tom Cringles Log* and the *Cruise of the Midge*, was born in 1789. It was also the mansion in which Charles Dickens stayed when he made his last visit to Glasgow in 1865. Balornock Mansion was the home of Andrew Menzies who was responsible for the tartan buses being the first City transport. Germiston House was built by Sir Robert Hamilton who owned this estate and was made a baronet of Nova Scotia in 1646. Possil Mansion was the home of Sheriff Allison, who was the author of *Allison's History of Europe*, which features an interesting account of Napoleon's privations during the retreat from Moscow.

Springburn can lay claim to the largest golf course in Glasgow. Littlehill Golf Course was opened in 1922 and was designed by James Braid, five times winner of the British Open Golf Championship. It has been said that, near the second tee, Auchinairn victims of the cholera plague of 1830–40 were buried. Nearby is Slaughterhouse Path, an old drovers' road.

Springburn is reputed to have had the first railway in Scotland, the Glasgow and Garnkirk Railway, which was opened in 1831. The opening was marked by the appearance of George Stephenson, a pioneer in steam locomotion, who actually drove one of the engines. This railway supplied coal to Charles Tennent's Chemical Works, Sighthill, which was founded in 1797 and which, in its day, was the largest of its kind in the world. Their main products were sulphuric acid, bleaching powder, soda ash, soda crystals and soap, and they excelled at making soap. A feature of Tennent's Chemical Works was the Tennent's Stack which was 453 feet high and a famous landmark. A plaque situated on the left hand side of

GARNKIRK RAILWAY OPENING, 1831

the underpath from Royston Road to Baird Street gives a brief history of this chemical work.

The North British Locomotive Works were formed by the union of three separate firms in 1903. They were the Hydepark Locomotive Works, founded in 1836 at Hydepark Street, Anderston, latterly moving to Springburn in 1862, Messrs. Sharp Roberts (the oldest firm) which was founded in 1833 in Manchester and which moved to Springburn as the Atlas Works, and Messrs. Dubs, founded in 1863, situated at Polmadie and known later as The Queen's Park Locomotive Works. In addition there were two Railway Locomotive Works, the Caledonian or St. Rollox, established 1856, which built locomotives for the old Caledonian Railway, and latterly the L.M.S. (London Midland and Scottish Railway) set up in 1923. The Cowlairs Locomotive Works was started in 1842 by the Edinburgh and Glasgow Railway Company only to be absorbed by the NORTH BRITISH RAILWAY in 1844. L.N.E.R. (London North Eastern Railway) took over the works in 1923 carrying on the tradition of making first class locomotives. The two mile long Cowlairs Incline, built in 1842, was considered an outstanding engineering achievement. The soil and rock excavated from the incline tunnel was used to fill in the declivities on nearby Sighthill.

The skilled craftsmen of Springburn, by their diligence and foresight, made Springburn the greatest steam locomotive metropolis in Europe, and it was well within their skills to build a giant locomotive weighing 220 tons. From all corners of the world came eager demands for locomotives made in Springburn.

The one time North British Locomotives are a silent reminder of the grandeur of old Springburn. The building is now the Springburn College of Engineering and is of beautiful red sandstone. Contained within its walls is much data reflecting the life of the staff of the North British Locomotive Works. There are three commemorative windows, unveiled by H.R.H. The Prince of Wales, Edward Albert, on 9th March 1921, depicting the armed services in which the staff were engaged during the 1914–18 war. A memorial inscription reads 'To commemorate the services of the 3020 men who joined the colours and of the other employees men and women who were engaged in the manufacture of munitions of war in the works in the North British Locomotive Company, 334 men were killed in the 1914–18 war'. The building was used as a Red Cross general hospital during that war. Another plaque, commemorating the historic opening of the North British Locomotive Headquarters, reads 'This building was formally opened by the Right Hon. the Earl of Roseberry. Archibald Philip Primrose K.G.K.T. Prime Minister and first Lord of the Treasury 1894–1895'. In his address at the opening ceremony Lord Roseberry said 'I am glad to see so great an enterprise as this. I can see nothing but good, the saving of waste. The concentration in the union of the three great firms that produce the same article and wish to produce it as economically as possible. You have joined forces to promote efficiency, you have made this building to promote efficiency and long may that word be your motto.'

In the Transport Museum at Albert Road, Glasgow, there are a number of Springburn-made steam locomotives on show. They include the Glen Douglas built at Cowlairs in 1913 for the West Highland Railway, and one built in the Atlas Works by Sharp, Stewart and Co. Limited in 1894. St. Rollox or Caledonian Works is represented by a locomotive built in their premises in 1899. There is also a locomotive bearing the military name 'Gordon Highlander' which was built for the Great North of Scotland Railway. The first electrified tramcar which ran from Mitchell Street to Springburn, which was affectionately known as a room and kitchen or but and ben, was built at Caplaw Hill and can also be seen at the museum.

A reminder of the opening of the Railways was discovered in 1929 when workmen, engaged in reconditioning the road at East Flemington Street, discovered 100 yards of old railway line complete with sleepers, chairs, spikes and keys one foot below the surface of the road. This line served a pottery, long since defunct, which was probably the Campbellfield Pottery (latterly known as Springburn Pottery Co.), Flemington Street. It manufactured Rockingham Ware and white earthenware.

David Bennie & Sons Ltd., 60 Hobden Street, was the oldest nail manufacturer in Glasgow, and in the immediate pre-war era manufactured ½ million tons of nails annually.

There were thousands of Irish navvies working in and around Springburn during the construction of the vast railway network. History records that two Irish navvies, Doolan and Redding, were hanged for killing their foreman ganger near Crosshill Farm, Bishopbriggs, in 1840. They were eventually hanged near the scene of the crime. It has been said that sometime after this incident two faces were sculptured on the railway cutting near Colston by the navvies in memory of Doolan and Redding. The sculptured work is not defaced and can be easily seen to this day. Not far from this point and close to the railway is a pets' cemetery obviously abandoned and now used as a dump, but a few of the headstones are still visible.

Cowlairs Co-operative Society, founded in 1881 just at the time when Springburn was emerging from a sleepy village to an important railway suburb of Glasgow, fittingly enough adopted a steam locomotive as its trademark. At the corner of Vulcan Street and Springburn Road stands a monument of red granite which states: Presented to the Corporation of Glasgow on the 22nd August 1902 by the Cowlairs Co-operative Society Limited on the occasion of the Society's coming of age. 1881–1902. There is of course the locomotive depicted with N.B.R. inscribed on the tender and also the two co-operative mottos: Each for all and all for each and Union is strength. Unfortunately the plaque from this monument has recently been taken away by vandals.

In order to produce the skilled craftsmen of which Springburn is justly proud it was necessary to provide good schools. A few anecdotes regarding some of these schools and other incidents could be mentioned. During the demolition of Govan's School, Balgrayhill (the oldest school in Springburn) two tawse were discovered and they are now on show at the People's Palace, Glasgow Green. A plaque was also found with the armorial bearings of the City of Glasgow. It was discovered attached to the doorway of a greenhouse in the Cowlairs Allotments for railway employees which were established in 1881. It was made of cast iron and mounted on an oak board with a latin inscription which is possibly pre-Reformation. This item is also on show at the People's Palace. Both items were found and gifted to the corporation by Mr. Henry McComish, a railway employee.

Old Mosesfield, built in 1795 at Bagnall Street, Balgrayhill, had the motto of Glasgow University, *Via Veritas Vita*, inscribed upon the pillars of the gateway suggesting that it had some association with the University. To substantiate this statement the Rev. Jack Stewart states that the University still draws £200 feu duty from the original lands of Balgray. Petershill School, opened in 1887 at 33 Petershill Road, is now known as Albert Secondary Annex, and has a proud educational record which they are pleased to display. The names written on the wall of the school in large letters are the names of 98 boys and girls who were each dux from 1895–1944. A tribute to the efficiency of Springburn education is the news that William Young, a pupil of Albert Secondary School, was the first boy in Scotland to win the Edith Woolfson Scholarship for Gordonstoun. Edith Woolfson is the wife of Sir Isaac Woolfson who was granted the freedom of Glasgow earlier this year. Young was also dux of Ferness Knockburn Primary School. Ian McDonald Laval, a sheet metal apprentice from 76 Horne Street, Springburn, won the coveted gold medal for the top apprentice of the world. Typical of the many new schools being built in Springburn is St. Aloysius Primary School at 12 Carron Street. It was opened by Councillor Peter Gemmell, B.L., in 1967.

There are many little odd corners in Springburn which are of intriguing interest and which in the near future will probably be demolished completely from the scene. The site for the library at 179 Ayr Street, which was opened in 1906, was gifted by Messrs. Nielson Reid & Co., Hydepark Locomotive Works. The derelict Hydepark Works lie opposite the library, and it has been stated that the dining room of the Hydepark works was the last dance hall in Springburn. Quin's Public House at 728 Springburn Road was opened in 1864 and is one of the oldest public houses in Springburn. Pre-1939 a feature of this public house was a little room beneath the stairs reserved exclusively for old customers and a little poem is still current regarding it. The chorus runs thus:

Down in the wee room under the stairs
Everybody's happy Everybody's there
All gay and merry each in his chair
Down in the wee room under the stairs.

At the foot of Balgrayhill was a row of weavers' cottages known as Waal Brae. They were demolished to make way for the children's pleasure ground which was a gift of Sir Hugh Reid. Opposite this point is the Balgray Café, 10 Balgrayhill, which has been this kind of establishment for as long as can be remembered. It is said that at one time water troughs for horses were situated near the door. It is reputed to be the oldest building in Springburn. It is rumoured that a toll house, demolished some years ago, stood opposite St. Rollox church at the corner of Fountainwell Road. The last person to live in the toll house was a Mr. Craig who was a cab hirer. Near this spot is the National Carriers Ltd., Sighthill Depot, which is built on the site of a quarry where the stones were hewn for the old Glasgow University which was situated at High Street, Glasgow. The first doctor to hold practice in Springburn was a Doctor Graham whose house at 77 Northcroft Road still stands.

The Corporation Baths and Washhouses opened in Kay Street in 1897. At the same time the Springburn Amateur Swimming Club was officially formed producing many promising swimmers among whom was John Service, Scottish breast stroke champion, and Robert Miller, Scottish free style champion and internationalist. It has been noted that a unique feature of the swimming baths is the presence of hundreds of sparrows who nest in the premises and feed on the abundance of cockroaches or steam beetles which infest the building. The Springburn Public Hall at 11

Millarbank Street is now a sports centre and a plaque in the vestibule of the building states: Sports Council for Glasgow. The Sports Centre opened on 31st October 1963 by The Rt. Hon. The Lord Provost Peter Meldrum Esqu. J.P. Convener – Andrew Convery, Sub Convener – Richard McCutcheon, Alexander Roche B.C., J.P. Town Clerk.

It is probably not too well known that Springburn has strong associations with Scotland's greatest warrior and patriot, William Wallace. A monument marking the site of the house where he was betrayed stands at the east end of Robroyston Road near Robroyston Mains Farm and on it is stated: 'This memorial erected 1900 A.D. by public subscriptions is to mark the site of the house in which the hero of Scotland was basely betrayed and captured about midnight on 5th August 1305 when along with his faithful friend and co-patron "Kerlie" who was slain.'

From the debris of Springburn has sprung up many fine multi-storied flats and not least is the 24-storey blocks at Balgrayhill Road. At Red Road are built the highest multis in Europe. It has been stated that two of the 32 multi blocks have the remarkable distinction of housing around 900 children, possibly the highest child density in Scotland or even Britain. The plaque, at Royston Square, was unveiled appropriately enough by Lord Provost Jean Roberts who was born in Springburn. This plaque was unveiled by The Rt. Hon. Lord Provost Mrs. Jean Roberts J.P. to commemorate the completion of the Royston Road Housing Development on the 10th August 1961.

The story of Springburn will roll on amidst the debris and chaos of a redevelopment area. The Springburn Association has been formed to provide a vital link with the past history of this famous district, and the author would wish to thank its members for their co-operation.

Langside

Langside Monument

Langside College, which is built on Clincart Hill, would hardly be considered today as the ideal vantage point to view a battle scene. If, however, the visitor was able to throw back the curtains of time some 403 years then the panorama of the famous Battle of Langside would present itself. Picture the scene:

It is a still morning at 9 o'clock, the tense moment before the battle. The soldiers on one side, chiefly Hamiltons, are led by the Fifth Earl of Argyle, Lieutenant of Scotland, with Lord Claude Hamilton commanding the first line. The cannon have been drawn up in suitable formation and the cavalry stand by ready for action with the horses impatiently snorting and pawing, their riders holding them gently but firmly in check, ready for the signal of their commander to engage in battle with the opposing troops. They have mustered under a young 26 year old woman who has been Queen of Scotland since she was a week old and who has also been for two years Queen of France. She has taken herself to the safety of Court Knowe, adjacent to Cathcart Castle, to view the battle.

Queen Mary of the Scots views, with apprehension, the other army in battle array and led by her half brother Regent Moray. It is stationed on the higher hill and with better coverage in the village of Langside. He has a smaller army of 3,000 to 4,000 men, including 600 men from the town of Glasgow and 200 of the Clan McFarlane whose chief, Andrew, Laird of Arrochar, had been condemned to die but had been pardoned.

In the ensuing battle, three of Mary's Standards are captured. They were kept for a long time, as relics, in the Laird's castle at Arrochar. The battle rages for three quarters of an hour. 300

of the Queen's troops are killed and many more die of wounds. The casualties on the Regent's side were comparatively slight but he forbids the slaughter of Queen Mary's fleeing troops. Mary, viewing the fateful scene from the Court Knowe (now marked by a memorial stone) took to her horse for a place of safety as this day her hopes of wearing the Crown of Scotland were dashed for ever. It is probable that Willie Douglas her liberator from Lochleven Castle, and one of her ladies-in-waiting, Mary Seton, were in her company as she fled from the battlefield.

Many of the dead of the battle were buried on the site of what is now the Queen's Park boating pond which was then a marsh. The marsh, for a long time, was considered haunted. Indeed, it is said that a lady residing in a lodge house at the entrance to the old Camphill Estate claims to have seen the spectres of soldiers rising from the mud and water.

Turning our eyes from the Battle of Langside, we scan the surrounding district and find we are standing on part of a rich coalfield which extends from the Trap Hills of Campsie in the north to Cathkin Braes in the south. There is also an abundance of ironstone of the best quality on the neighbouring estate of Linn and a freestone quarry in Crosshill.

A great deal of controversy surrounds the derivation of the name of adjacent Mount Florida. A newspaper account of 1819 refers to Mount Floradale later known as Mount Floridan. A house in this district in days gone by was known as Mount Florida House and was occupied by an American family who perhaps had some connection with the ancient tobacco lords of Glasgow. The name of Bolivar Terrace commemorates the liberator of South America; a tablet fixed at the entrance to No. 16 Bolivar Terrace confirms this.

The Cathcart family were prominent in the district and the ancient edifice of Cathcart Castle, now a picturesque ruin in the Linn Park, was their fortress. In the year 1513 three of the family fell at Flodden Field and a nephew fell at the Battle of Pinkie in 1547. The Fifth Earl of Cathcart commanded the military at the Battle of Copenhagen in 1807. He was the superior officer of the Duke of Wellington and two of his sons fought at the Battle of Waterloo in 1815.

In the district of Newlands small earthenware pots filled with coins were found, and it is thought they were planted by a cavalier of fortune, Dugald Dalgetty, who, returning from service on the continent, got involved in the struggles of his native land and for some reason was unable to collect his treasure.

A great deal of conjecture has arisen about what type of camp existed at Camphill. It has been labelled as a Roman Camp and also a Prehistoric Camp but in the light of recent excavations, carried out in 1951, it is thought to have been a Camp built during the English Invasions of the 13th and 14th centuries and was purely medieval. A beautiful Roman vase, now in the Huntarian Museum was, however, found in the district, and a Roman coin was found at a local Bowling Green. The circle of stones, situated on the crown of the camp, long thought to have historical significance, were, according to an eye witness, placed there 75 years ago by workmen building a road nearby.

Many of the well-known families have disappeared from the district but existing names of streets, etc., still carry the memory. Blairs of Aitkenhead, Sir John Maxwell of Pollok, Graham of Dripps, Brown of Langside, Thomson of Camphill and Clark of Crosshill.

It is interesting to note some of the old industries which existed in the district. In 1690, a paper mill was set up by a Huguenot, Nicholas de Shan, and there were the Bleachfield at Newlands and the Netherlee Print Mill. The old Snuff Mill's bridge, built 347 years ago, crosses the Cart and was an important stage coach route to Ayr and the South. In 1786, Robert Burns trod over the bridge on his way to Glasgow in an attempt to sell the first editions of his poems. Unsuccessful, he tramped his weary way back to Kilmarnock.